The Little Orange Handbook 2.0

The Netherlands for Newcomers

Tulip Fields near Noordwijk

Kralingse Bos, Rotterdam

Woodland, Velsen-Noord

Contents

About the Netherlands

The Netherlands in a Nutshell

The Dutch Culture

The Dutch Language

Living in the Netherlands

Your First Steps

Working in the Netherlands

Money matters

A Place to Stay

Education

Getting Around

Health Care

Nieuwe Waterweg, Hoek van Holland

Introduction

Dear reader,

Welcome to the second edition of *The Little Orange Handbook*! This handy guide to life in the Netherlands provides you with practical tips and hints for living here as well as a compact cultural, historical and economic background on Dutch society and its people's mentality. Just take a quick peek at the table of contents for a first impression of the highly useful stuff waiting for you to explore.

Whether they be expats or foreign students, migrants usually concentrate on the cities – and most Dutch cities are quite attractive and offer plenty of things to do. In their historical centers, a rich cultural life flourishes and there are attractions for all tastes and wallets. Many Dutch urbanites are cosmopolitan people with liberal worldviews and sometimes rather unconventional lifestyles, who find themselves rubbing shoulders with others who have more limited views on modern society. And often just 40 kilometers separate these cities from insular villages with strict religious traditions and other forms of conservatism.

Speaking of the countryside; away from cities and high-

ways, the Netherlands has quite a lot to offer in the field of charming scenery and natural beauty, with quiet country roads and wide panoramas in which water is the dominant factor.

Staying in the Netherlands longer than the average tourist would will make you aware of the pros and cons of living here. On the plus-side, most visitors experience society as being relaxed and open; transparent, and welcoming to new ideas and new people. There is great political and personal autonomy in the Netherlands, with freedom of press, religion and opinion. The Dutch make ample use of this freedom, as you will certainly find after learning the language (though their ability to express their opinions in English is just fine, too). Or just by turning on the news – witness the protests organized by the Dutch farmers in 2022 regarding the environmental measures the Dutch government wanted to introduce, leading the farmers to take to the highways in their tractors, dump hay and put up barricades. Keeping Dutch directness in mind, you will inevitably also hear less pleasant ideas and some extreme opinions, but it is up to you whether you want to go into debate over them or not. Still, whatever your personal lifestyle or your preferences regarding religion, sexuality, politics, etcetera, are; in the Netherlands you can live in accordance with them – provided you respect other people's choices as well...

Kralingse Plas, Rotterdam

Other plusses when it comes to life here, are the excellent quality of health care and education, both of which rank very high in world statistics. This book will inform you of some of the particularities when it comes to how it all works, just to help you on your way. Likewise, the country is seen as child-friendly: children are both loved and taken seriously and there are numerous venues in which tomorrow's adult citizens can enjoy themselves and develop their skills. Think of museums and theaters, but also of fun parks and child-friendly restaurants.

For children and adults alike, the Dutch sports scene is also very diverse. There are thousands of sports clubs, most of which have excellent facilities. These facilities, both indoors and outdoors, are to be found everywhere, and in this country known for its plentiful water, all kinds of water sports are popular and well-facilitated. Sports clubs usually also welcome people from 'outside' – even those who do not yet speak the local language – so membership may be a good way to make new friends.

Moreover, life here leaves you time to enjoy it all. The Dutch are a hardworking lot, but they also highly value leisure time. Official workweeks for employees are less than 40 hours, but of course the self-employed and people in leading positions make longer hours. Even so, they enjoy several weeks of holidays and succeed in spending most evenings and weekends with their loved ones. 'Quality time' is not a hot topic here, but Dutch society is certainly not '24/7', and people from more hectic economies can initially be annoyed by this – though most of them find themselves adjusting 'surprisingly' well to a life less stressful.

Less favorable comments on life in the Netherlands usually remark on the many rules and regulations – written but also unwritten ones. Other complaints concern the individualism of the Dutch: the downside of personal freedom is that people may leave you to your own devices. True friendship is a long-term thing in Dutch culture, involving a slow approach with increasingly personal conversation. The Dutch prefer their friends to share certain basic ideas on life and lifestyle, so people from outside need to 'work their way in'. Speaking Dutch will obviously help, but the good news and the bad news is that just about all

Dutch people speak English and they almost automatically switch to it as soon as they hear you slowly stumble your way through Dutch. This may be good for fast understanding but not for improving your language skills!

Two other issues that have incurred negative commentary have been how the government dealt with COVID-19 – including inconsistent advice on masks, poor anticipation of the need for subsequent lockdowns, a slow start of the vaccination program, combined of course with the Dutch attitude that no one should tell them what to do – and how the government dealt with the influx of Ukrainian refugees after the Russian invasion of Ukraine in 2022. Due to a lack of beds for these refugees, up to 250 of them found themselves sleeping outside in the late summer, while the hygiene in the centers was sub-par. These events, plus a few others, have led to a drop in confidence in Dutch politics, however, as political pundits say; this has happened before, it has always recovered, and all things are relative – causing them to see no reason for concern.

Quite a few visitors comment on old-fashioned attitudes regarding male-female role patterns: most Dutch women are strong, independent and quite successful, but certain economic and cultural factors may hold them down, obviously a matter under debate.

A final criticism is that the Dutch tend to be rather money-oriented. Even though they may be less thrifty than before, price and 'usefulness' are still important factors in any decision, while more romantic notions such as esthetics, style or fashionability come second.

Overall, the Netherlands is a good place to be, and this book will help you settle in, whether you are an expat, an international student, a love immigrant or any other kind of long-term visitor. Let me conclude by saying: welcome to the Netherlands!

Jacob Vossestein

Jacob is a former cross-cultural trainer at KIT, Amsterdam and author of the international bestseller *Dealing with the Dutch*

About the
Netherlands

Years of History

200,000 BC	The first site to generate human remains: a homo erectus camp. For dinner they had dwarf rhino
120,000 BC	Neanderthals
5300 BC	The first agricultural settlement in southern Netherlands
3500 BC	Era of the people that constructed the dolmens (*Hunebedden*)
2200 BC	Stone starts being replaced by copper and later bronze
700 BC	Start of the Iron Age
57 BC–402 AD	The Romans conquer the country. The Rhine becomes their border. Cities: Nijmegen, Voorburg
400-800	After the fall of the Roman Empire, the Frisian create their own kingdom north of the Rhine. It shares a border with the large Frankish empire, which in the end comprises the entire territory of the current country of the Netherlands. Conversion to Christianity
800-1000	Invasions of the Normans. Creation of independent counties and duchies, which lay at the basis of most of the current provinces

Dolmens (*Hunebedden*)

1214 Dordrecht is the first city north of the Meuse and the Rhine to acquire city rights. Ultimately, these are awarded to many cities in the Netherlands

1421 Saint Elisabeth Flood. Creation of the Biesbosch

1396–1467 Philip the Good, Duke of Burgundy unites most of the counties and duchies of the Netherlands under his reign

1477 Great privilege. The cities, nobility and clergy of the Netherlands recognize Mary of Burgundy, granddaughter of Philip the Good, as their Duchess if she honors their rights and privileges. This boils down to her having to rule the area in collaboration with them. Comparable to England's Magna Charta. Predecessor to the Constitution

1568 Battle of Heiligerlee, and the start of the 80-Year War and uprising against Philip II of Spain, Mary's heir. This uprising is in protest against the loss of privileges and rights, as well as against the persecution of the Protestants. The revolt is led by William of Orange

1584 William of Orange is shot to death by a terrorist contracted by Philip II

1602 Establishment of the United East India Company, one of the earliest companies that is financed by

The Romans conquer the country

Willam of Orange is shot to death

means of shares and, for more than a century, by far the largest multinational in the world. Start of the Golden Age

1607 Twelve-Year Truce between Spain and the insurgents. Spain recognizes the independence of the Republic of Seven United Provinces or Seven United Netherlands, which had already been proclaimed by the insurgents in 1588

1648 Definitive peace with Spain

1779 The Republic of Seven United Netherlands recognizes the United States. This leads to the start of a war with England in 1780. John Adams is the first representative of the United States in the Netherlands

1795 Towards the end of the 18th century, the century of decline, a French army occupies the Netherlands. The federal and feudal Republic of Seven United Netherlands becomes the Batavian Republic: a united state, with modern legislation and a modern government

1806 Napoleon appoints his brother Louis King of Holland

1810 Napoleon annexes the Kingdom of Holland

1813 Revolt against the rule of Napoleon. William I is declared sovereign ruler and then King in 1815. The north and south Netherlands are united. The French reforms are maintained

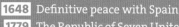

Philip II

First railroad, 1839

1830 Revolt in Brussels. Belgium secedes

1839 First railroad tracks are laid, between Amsterdam and Haarlem

1848 New constitution. From now on, the ministers are accountable to a directly elected parliament. The King is inviolable

1866 Nieuwe Waterweg is created. This connects Rotterdam with the sea, allowing it to become the largest harbor in Europe

1914–1918 The Netherlands remains neutral during the First World War

1917 Introduction universal suffrage for men – two years later, for women. The Netherlands becomes a democracy. A government is created in which Christian politicians dominate. Christian politicians remain in all Dutch cabinets until 1993

1919 Founding Royal Dutch Airlines (Koninklijke Luchtvaart Maatschappij, KLM), based from the home airport of Schiphol near Amsterdam

1940–1945 German occupation

1948 The Netherlands joins NATO

1949 The Netherlands recognizes Indonesia's independence, proclaimed by the country itself in 1945

1951 Start of the boom and a period of quick economic growth that goes on until the 1970s. The Netherlands is a founding member of the European Coal and Steel Community

German occupation, 1940–1945

Liberation 1945

1953	North Sea Flood. As disastrous as the Saint Elisabeth Flood
1954	Decision to implement the Delta Plan, aimed at forever avoiding another disaster such as the one in 1953
1957	The Netherlands is a founding member of the Euro market, precursor of the European Union
1963	The Netherlands grants New Guinea to Indonesia
1973	First energy crisis, followed by a recession
1975	Surinam becomes independent
1979	Second energy crisis, followed by the economic crisis of the '80s
1993	For the first time since 1917, a cabinet is formed without Christian politicians, in which liberals and social-democrats work together. Era of an economic boom, stimulated by the ICT market
1995	Blood bath in Srbrenica: Serbian militia slaughter 6,000 Muslim men in Bosnia, in an area that should have been under the protection of Dutch UN troops
2002	Murder of populist Pim Fortuyn. This constitutes the second time that a Dutch politician is shot to death. The first was William of Orange
2008	Due to the credit crisis, the Dutch government has to save the country's largest banks – ABN Amro

North Sea Flood in Zeeland, 1953

and ING – with the help of heavy financial injections. ABNAmro is nationalized. The housing market starts to collapse. Increasing unemployment. Modest recovery only starts in 2014/2015.

2010 The Dutch Antilles cease to exist. Sint Maarten and Curaçao become autonomous countries within the Kingdom of the Netherlands. Saba, Bonaire and Sint Eustatius become municipalities of the Netherlands.

2013 Queen Beatrix abdicates. The Netherlands has a new king and queen; Willem-Alexander and Máxima.

2014 On July 17, a Malaysia Air airplane, carrying 283 people, of whom 196 are Dutch, is shot down over Ukraine by Russian military equipment.

2020 The Covid-19 pandemic strikes, leading to three (partial and total) lockdowns, and claiming over 22,000 lives.

2021 The assassination of crime journalist Peter R. de Vries on July 15 in Amsterdam

2022 Months long protests organized by large groups of Dutch farmers regarding the environmental measures the Dutch government wanted to introduce.

Energy crisis, 1973

The Netherlands in a Nutshell

The Hague

The Dutch Political System

I t took a while for the various peoples of Europe to rid themselves of their absolute monarchs, but eventually also the
Dutch managed to make the Netherlands a constitutional monarchy. In a constitutional monarchy,
the constitution determines how
the powers are divided between the
monarch and the other institutions
of the government.

The person of the
King is inviolable.
The ministers are
responsible for
everything he does
or says. This creates
a delicate situation;
the King, the Queen
and their princesses
cannot make any
public statements
without consulting
with the Prime
Minister first.

The Cabinet

If you have been following
Dutch politics for a while, you may
have noticed that the number of
ministers tends to change from one
cabinet to the next. This can happen
for a variety of reasons, such as the
introduction of a new post that is
considered sufficiently important
under the current circumstances to
warrant its own minister. Or in order to ensure that the numeric
distribution of the members of the cabinet reflects the represen-
tation of the coalition partners in the Parliament as closely as it
can, so that none of the coalition partners feels sold short.

The Parliament

The Netherlands has a representative democracy and its
Parliament (*Staten Generaal*) is made up of two chambers: the
Upper House (*Eerste Kamer*), whose 75 members are elected by
the members of the provincial councils; and the Lower House
(*Tweede Kamer,* or Second Chamber), whose 150 members are
elected directly by the people.

The Netherlands has a system of proportional representa-
tion. Voters vote for a party that submits a list of candidates, but

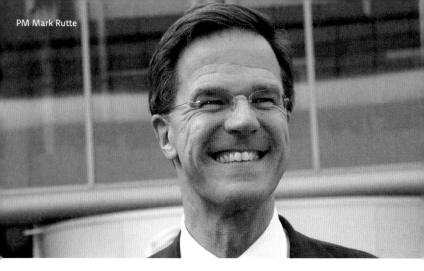

they can also vote for a particular candidate; those who receive more than 25 percent of the party's quota for a seat are guaranteed a seat in the Parliament. The other seats are divided according to the order in which the party candidates appear on the list.

The elections for the Second Chamber and the Upper House do not take place simultaneously; they are separated by a number of years. This means that a government can have a majority in the Second Chamber, without having one in the First.

The Provincial States

The provinces, of which there are 12, each have their own government, which consists of three bodies: the Provincial States (Provinciale Staten), the Provincial Executive (Gedeputeerde Staten) and the King's Commissioner (Commissaris van de Koning). The King's Commissioner presides over the States-General and the Provincial Executive, and is appointed for a term of six years. The Provincial Executive is elected from members of the Provincial States and is charged with the overall management of the province. The Provincial States – sometimes referred to as the States General, but that is confusing as there is also a States General of the Netherlands, which is the parliament – is the provincial parliament, which is elected every four years in direct elections and largely from the same political parties as the national elec-

tions. Once the Provincial States have been elected, they elect the members of the Upper House within three months.

Municipal Councils

Every four years, the inhabitants of the Dutch cities and towns vote for their municipal council. The smallest councils have nine members, the largest, 45. The municipal councils occupy themselves with social services, health care, traffic, public schooling, housing, etc.

The Political Parties

There are ten sizeable parties that have been around for a reasonable period of time, varying from since 1918 (the SGP, or Reformed Political Party), to since 2006 (the PVV, or Party for Freedom). However, there are several more parties that have sprung up over recent years, as well as parties that cannot be found in the national government, but that can be found in municipal or provincial governments.

In the past, politics used to be a lot more straightforward than now. There were three large parties that were effectively in control. The socialists (PvdA – Labor Party), the Christians and the Catholics (CDA – Christen-Democratisch Appèl) and the Liberals (VVD – Volkspartij voor Vrijheid en Democratie). Since the creation of political parties, one of these three parties (or their predecessors) has supplied the country's Prime Minister. In 2022, the leader of the latter party, Mark Rutte, had in fact been Prime Minister for ten years.

Due to a series of party splits, the introduction of one-issue parties (animal rights, racism, farmers), coupled with a tilt to the right, the political smorgasbord has become more diverse than ever. This has also made the political landscape somewhat unpredictable, because in order to achieve a majority, you need to bring together a multitude of parties. These types of coalitions are hard to forge, which was illustrated by the aftermath of the 2021 national elections; it took almost a year to put together a cabinet that could be presented to King and country.

The following (20!) parties are in the parliament

→ **VVD** (Volkspartij voor Vrijheid en Democratie), 34 seats, conservative liberal
→ **D66** (Democraten 66), 24 seats, social liberal
→ **PVV** (Partij voor de Vrijheid), 17 seats, right liberalists
→ **CDA** (Christen-Democratisch Appèl), 14 seats, Christian democrat
→ **SP** (Socialistische Partij), 8 seats, social
→ **PvdA** (Partij van de Arbeid), 9 seats, social democrat
→ **GL** (Groenlinks), 8 seats, green
→ **PvdD** (Partij voor de Dieren), 6 seats, animal rights
→ **CU** (ChristenUnie), 5 seats, Christian democrat
→ **FVD** (Forum voor Democratie), 5 seats, right-wing populist, national conservatist
→ **JA21**, 3 seats, conservatist
→ **SGP** (Staatkundig Gereformeerde Partij), 3 seats, religious right
→ **DENK**, 3 seats, minority rights
→ **Volt Nederland**, 2 seats, European federalist
→ **BBB** (BoerenBurgerBeweging), 1 seat, agrarian
→ **BIJ1**, 1 seat, intersectional
→ **BVNL**, 3 seats, right-wing populist, national conservatist
→ **Fractie Den Haan**, 1 seat, party for the elderly
→ **Lid Gündoğan**, 1 seat, social liberal
→ **Lid Omtzigt**, 1 seat, christian democrat

Forming a Cabinet

Because there are so many political parties in the Netherlands, there are numerous coalition possibilities. Consequently, after the elections, the Lower House appoints a so-called *informateur*, whose task it is to investigate which political parties could be brought together to create a coalition cabinet. He advises the King on his outcome, who asks this *informateur* – or a new one – to meet with the leaders of the parties that constitute the most viable coalition in order to discuss the government's program and ministerial posts. This leads to a coalition agreement concept, which is reported to the King. This concept includes the name of a *formateur* who is to lead the formation of the coalition government and who often becomes Minister President. He is appointed to do this by the Lower House.

> The Netherlands also has Water Boards, which are responsible for flood control and water resources management.

Voting

Anyone who wants to vote in the Netherlands must be 18 years of age.

If you are an **EU citizen**, you can vote in municipal elections if you are a resident of a particular municipality on the day on which the candidates are nominated. You can vote for the Water Boards if you live in a 'watership'. To vote for the European Parliament you must be an EU citizen, a resident of the Netherlands, and you may not vote in the same election in your home country, nor be disqualified from voting here or in your home country.

As a **Non-EU citizen**, you can vote in municipal elections if you have been a legal resident of the Netherlands for a continuous period of at least five years, and you can vote for Water Boards if you live in a 'watership' and are a legal resident of the Netherlands.

Only **Dutch nationals** may vote in elections for the Lower House of the Parliament and the Provincial States.

The Royal Family

While the British Royal Family is closing the lightyears-wide gap between the British Royal family and the public, the Dutch Royal Family is far ahead of them. Queen Wilhelmina, seen as the matriarch of the Netherlands, was loved by the people, politicians and the army, and esteemed by political adversaries. Also her daughter, Queen Juliana, was seen as a kindhearted personality whom people looked up to but loved at the same time. Queen Beatrix, though somewhat more formal, was always greatly respected, and King Willem-Alexander is not only warm, but also youthful and relaxed – more in keeping with modern times and therefore more relatable.

Every now and then, the Netherlands goes through a phase in which calls go up for an abolition of the Royal Family, but the fact remains that the members of this Family are considered so pleasant, politically unobtrusive and inoffensive, as well as warm and modest, that opponents of the Royal Family simply cannot get enough support and the movement fizzles out again.

The Members

The Dutch Royal Family and the 'Royal House' are not the same. Not every member of the Orange Nassau family is a member of the Royal House. The Royal Family is made up of the former Queen and her sisters, their spouses and their children, King Willem-Alexander, his brothers, their spouses and their children and grandchildren. Who becomes a member of the Royal *House* – and therefore could theoretically become the monarch – has been determined by law and consists of the Head of State King Willem-Alexander, his wife Queen Máxima, their children and their spouses and grandchildren, his mother (formerly Queen Beatrix), as well as his brother Prince Constantijn and his wife Princess Laurentien, and his aunt Princess Margriet and her husband Pieter van Vollenhoven.

Members of the Royal House who marry without the official approval of the Parliament, lose the right to succeed to the Throne. When then-Prince Willem-Alexander announced his

The Dutch
Royal Family

Queen Máxima

intention to marry Máxima Zorreguieta of Argentina, there was an iffy moment there, as there was some objection to Máxima's father's possible role in the Argentinean junta from 1976-1983 – but it was decided that though he may have been aware of what was going on, he could not be considered a participant and the couple was given the green light. This has, without a doubt, given the Dutch Royal Family a boost, as Máxima has been well-accepted by the public as an easy-going, respectable, dedicated Queen – and mother of three princesses: Catharina-Amalia (2003), Alexia (2005) and Ariana (2007).

Political Position

The King, together with the ministers, form the government. It was determined in 1848 that the ministers, and not the King, are responsible for acts of government. Laws that have been passed by the Parliament, and Royal Decrees, are signed by both the King (Queen, depending on who is at the head of the Royal House) and the minister in question, lending them the authority of the Head of State but placing the responsibility for them with the minister.

Prince's Day

Every year, on the third Tuesday of September, called *Prinsjesdag*, the King and members of his family ride in the royal "Glass" Coach from the palace on the Noordeinde to the Binnenhof, where the government is housed. Here the King holds his famous speech, called the *Troonrede*, before the members of the Upper and Lower House, in which the government's policies for the coming year are set out. *Prinsjesdag* is a popular outing for schools, but also for grown-ups and tourists, who come to The Hague to admire the beauty of the royal procession and taste a bit of the atmosphere of yesteryear.

King's Day

The very first 'regent's day', called Princess Day, was held on August 31, 1895 – in honor of Princess Wilhelmina's fifth birthday. The initiative to organize this was taken by the editor of an Utrecht newspaper, who wanted to celebrate the unity of the

Netherlands. It became a national tradition, with the date following the birthdays of the reigning monarchs: April 30 for Queen Juliana, and now April 27 for King Willem-Alexander. Queen Beatrix, though her birthday is on January 31, had left it on April 30, her mother's birthday, as she decided that the chances of a pleasant day of sunshine were considerably greater on that date.

Almost every municipality has an 'Orange Association' of diehard monarchists, who like to arrange a number of festivities that involve a lot of folklore and children's games. Wherever you go, you hear the thump of marching bands and other music. In Amsterdam, people come together to sell their secondhand items on the so-called Free Market (*Vrijmarkt*). This custom has spread across the nation the past 30 years, meaning that you will likely run into your neighbors' kids selling their old toys from makeshift stands, being a table or an old rug on the street. They will be flanked by grown-ups who are selling old percolators and other household items for a song. The King and his family visit one municipality on that day – giving the Orange Association the chance to go all out and organize a program of entertainment and fun for the King and his family.

Website
→ The Dutch Royal Family: www.Royal-House.nl

King's Day

Climate

Unfortunately, the Netherlands simply does not have the most exciting of climates. Granted, there are magnificent winter and glorious summer days but, sadly, not very many. This can be very hard to take for those who have not grown up here (and even for those who have!). Many expats comment on how the gray and dreary skies and constant rainfall make it all that much harder to be motivated to get out of bed in the morning and that the only thing that makes it even harder in the winter is that the sun comes up so late. So, what are the facts and how do you get through this?

> Approximately a quarter of the Netherlands lies below sea level.

Maritime Climate

Thanks to its location right on the North Sea, the Netherlands has a temperate maritime climate with relatively mild winters, mild summers and rain all year round. The Dutch gener-

Terminals Port of Rotterdam seen from beach town Kijkduin

ally feel that it rains a lot here, but statistics say differently. Approximately 7 percent of the time, there is some type of precipitation, such as rain, snow or hail – which translates into 100 minutes of precipitation a day, or 700-800 mm a year. It just feels as is its always raining because there is hardly a day on which the meteorologists can guarantee that it won't rain. But that doesn't mean it will.

Looking for something to talk about? Bring up the weather; it is sure to guarantee a conversation that will last as long as you need to fill the time.

→ Average daytime temperature in winter: 2-6° C
→ Average daytime temperature in summer: 17-20° C
→ The winter of 2015-2016 was the warmest in 300 years, with an average temperature of 9.9° C
→ The Summer of 2018 was the warmest summer in more than three centuries. The average temperature was 18.9° C against 17.0° C normal
→ Since 1910, there have been 61 storms with winds between 90 and 122 km/h
→ Between now and 2085, the sea level can rise anywhere between 25 and 85 cm

Global Warming

Is there really such a thing as global warming and is the Netherlands suffering the consequences? Who can really say? After all, temperatures have been rising since the end of the last ice age, as have the sea levels. During the ice ages, the sea level is generally 110 meters lower than now. However, during the Cretaceous, it was 220 m higher. In other words, world temperatures and, unavoidably linked to this, sea levels, fluctuate. Research has shown that the sea level around the Netherlands has risen by 3 millimeters a year over the past decades; 1.5 times the rate of the previous century. Nonetheless, this rate lies below the world average, which, apparently, is largely due to (storm)winds along the coast. Furthermore, the annual amount of precipitation has risen by 26 percent over the past 100 years.

The Netherlands Without Dikes

The Netherlands literally means Low Lands: 40% of this nation's land lies below sea level. Dunes, dikes, dams and delta works protect us against the water of the sea and the rivers. Without these barriers, the Netherlands would become largely immersed under water.

Leeuwarden Groningen

Assen

Lelystad Zwolle

Amsterdam

The Hague Utrecht

Arnhem

NORTH SEA Rotterdam

's-Hertogenbosch

GERMANY

Middelburg

Storms

Which doesn't mean that the Dutch shouldn't protect their land against floods – because if there is one thing history has shown, it is that the Netherlands is rightly worried about them, with the oldest recorded flood taking place in 838. In 1219, one of the most disastrous took place, which affected the provinces of Noord-Holland, Zuid-Holland and Friesland, as well as England and Germany, and which created the Zuiderzee (now known as the IJsselmeer), and the Wadden Sea.

The storm that is most engraved in the collective memories of the Dutch is that of 1953, when 1,800 people in Zeeland drowned and 100,000 people lost their homes. In one single night, 165,000 hectares of land were covered by sea. The storm really delivered a double whammy, however, when on the day after the first floods, the tide came back in again along with strong winds, and took the lives of the same number of people as it had taken during the first night.

The most recent surge was in 2007, when a storm caused the sea level to go up to 327 cm higher than NAP (Normaal Amsterdams Peil, or Amsterdam Ordnance Datum; the average summer flood level water in the IJ-River north of Amsterdam). The NAP is used as the reference point for water levels not only in the Netherlands, but also in Finland, Sweden, Norway and Germany.

Measures Against Flooding

The country's most famous measure against flooding is the Delta Works, which – though the plans were already on the table before – can be considered the direct consequence of the storm of 1953. They have been created to protect the provinces of Zeeland, Zuid-Holland and Noord-Brabant. Construction started towards the end of the 1960s and it was completed in 1986. It cost approximately 2.5 billion euros and is supposed to reduce the chance of the recurrence of a flood to once every 4,000 years. The American Society of Civil Engineers have declared these works one of the seven modern world wonders.

Other large-scale measures are the relocation of the dikes in order to broaden the Waal River north of Nijmegen city center, and the Hollandse IJsselkering, meant to protect the lowest part of the Netherlands, which is located 6.76 m below NAP. On average, water levels cause the two 480 ton valves to be lowered into the river three times a year.

Websites
Weather forecast
→ www.drops.live
→ www.knmi.nl
→ www.weeronline.nl
→ www.weerplaza.nl
→ www.weathernews.nl

Rain forecast
→ www.buienalarm.nl
→ www.buienradar.nl

Pollen news
→ www.hooikoortsradar.nl

Religion

Although modern Dutch society is very secular, and 49 percent of the Dutch people identify with an organized religion, you will find plenty of churches and other places of worship, and you will have plenty of opportunity to practice your own religion if you wish.

The southern provinces of Brabant and Limburg are predominantly Catholic, and the other provinces are predominantly Protestant. Of the Dutch people who nowadays claim church affiliation, only about 5 percent of the population attends services regularly, and though there are more registered members of the Roman Catholic Church (4.1 million) than of the Protestant Church (2.7 million), only 17 percent of the Catholics go to church regularly, while 46.8 percent of the Protestants do.

With approximately 872,000 (practicing) Muslims living in the Netherlands (5 percent of the population), Islam has become one of the country's main religions. Mosques have been built in most of the larger cities by communities of immigrants from Turkey, Morocco and Indonesia, and the Dutch public is gradually learning more about Islam – enough to make allowances for colleagues and pupils who are fasting for Ramadan, for example.

IJsselmeer dikes near Wierum, Friesland

Only 13 percent of the Jewish population of the Netherlands, compared to almost 16 percent before the Second World War. Approximately a quarter of the Jewish population survived the war (38,200) and their numbers remain approximately the same. Most of them live in the center is in Amsterdam, though synagogues can also be found in other cities.

- → 55 percent not religious
- → 20 percent Roman Catholic
- → 15 percent Protestant
- → 5 percent Muslim
- → 5 percent other (Hindu, Buddhist, Jehovah's Witness, etc.)

Finding a Place of Worship

In Amsterdam, you can find several English-language church services, also in non-denominational churches, as well as synagogues, mosques, a Buddhist temple and a Hindu temple. On the site of www.iamsterdam.com you will find a list of English-language religious services in Amsterdam. On www.moskee-wijzer.nl you will find an overview of all mosques in the Netherlands. And on the site of www.expatica.com you will find a guide of English-language religious services in the Netherlands.

Wester Moskee, Amsterdam

Economy

The Netherlands is in the world's top ten in export volume and it ranks in the world's top twenty for GNP, even though it is one of the smallest countries of the world. It owes this favorable ranking, among others, to its advanced transportation infrastructure, the port of Rotterdam (the largest European seaport in the world in terms of container activity) and Schiphol Airport (the third largest airport in Europe), as well as its advanced telecom infrastructure, extensive (high-speed) railway network and central geographic location.

Randstad

After Paris, London and Milan, the Randstad (the area including, and between, Amsterdam, The Hague, Rotterdam and Utrecht) is the largest economic urban area in the EU, measured in terms of gross domestic product. This is due to the strong presence of financial and commercial services; which happens to be one of the motors of Dutch economy.

Sectors

The trade, hospitality and transportation accounts for approximately 21 percent of the Netherlands' GNP, followed by services (15 percent). Furthermore, the world's largest chemical companies are based here, while the Netherlands is one of Europe's largest suppliers of high-tech goods for both the industrial and the consumer market. It is also Europe's second-largest producer of natural gas, while Rotterdam imports and refines huge amounts of crude oil that is shipped to the rest of western Europe. Thanks to these offshore installations and refineries, the Netherlands has many activities in the oil and gas industries, including a strong research and development technology and a specialized construction industry.

As for employment: The commercial services sector remains the largest employer in the Netherlands, and has been for several years, closely followed by the health care and manufacturing industries. Also the trade, transport, financial services and information technology sectors are attracting an increasing amount of employees, and science & engineering is showing a constant and steadily increasing need for international and capable workers in areas such as water management, green and renewable energy, as well as logistics.

The Economy in Numbers

- Almost half the value of Dutch exports, which themselves amount to a total of 843 billion euros, is generated by the throughput of goods that arrive from abroad and are exported almost immediately
- 211 billion euros of services are exported and 201 billion euros of services are imported
- Approximately 33 percent of the production of electricity is generated by solar panels, windmills and biomass

Weena, Rotterdam

- The Netherlands is truly a throughput country. In 2021, the total cargo traffic of the Port of Rotterdam was 470 million tons. Inland navigation transported 370 million tons. Trains transported 42 million tons of goods
- 15 percent of the value of imports comes from Germany
- 3.5 percent of the Dutch households has 1 million euros or more
- Generally, it takes 10 days to meet the legal requirements for setting up a new business
- 17 percent of the Dutch population has been a victim of cyber-crime
- Medium to small-sized companies generate 63 percent of the value of Dutch exports
- The number of female part-time workers is twice as high in the Netherlands as it is in the EU-15
- On average, in the Netherlands women earn 13 percent less than men. This is less than the EU-average (15 percent)
- 40 percent of mothers stops working or works less once their first child is born
- There are 1.6 million companies in sole proprietorship; 1.1 million of these have 0 employees (just the owner) (also known as ZZP, or *zelfstandige zonder personeel*)
- There are almost 100,000 consultancies in the Netherlands
- 35 percent of the Dutch would rather work for themselves than for a boss
- 73 percent of employed women has a part-time job
- 64 percent of women is economically independent
- The Netherlands has 11.4 million pigs, almost 4 million heads of cattle, 850,000 sheep, 480,000 dairy goats ... and 100 million chickens

Websites
→ Statistics Netherlands (CBS): www.cbs.nl
→ De Nederlandsche Bank (DNB): www.dnb.nl

Financial District Zuidas, Amsterdam

the Netherlands

→ The Dutch drink an average of 83 liters of beer a year

→ The Netherlands is protected by 80,000 kilometers of dikes

→ The Dutch eat an average of 2 kilos of licorice (*drop*) a year

→ Not even 25 percent of the Dutch women give birth at home

→ Cheese has been made in the Netherlands since 400 AD

→ Has the highest percentage of part-time employees in the EU

→ There are 1,220 operational windmills in the Netherlands

→ On average, a Dutchman cycles 2.5 km a day and 1,100 km per year

→ There are more bicycles than people in the Netherlands: approximately 23 million, 5 million of which are electric

→ According UNICEF the Netherlands is the best country to grow up in for kids

→ The Netherlands has the highest percentage of Internet connections in Europe

→ With 517 people per km² the Netherlands has the highest population density in Europe

→ KLM is the oldest national airline in the world

→ Philips produced the first cassettes, video tapes, CDs and CD ROMs

→ The United East India Company was the first multinational corporation in the world and it was the first company to issue stocks

→ The microscope, telescope and thermometer are Dutch inventions

→ One out of three Dutch residents is a member of a sports club

→ 20 percent of all tweets in the world originate in the Netherlands

→ The letter E is the most-used letter in the Dutch language

→ The sports bra is a Dutch invention

→ On average five people are struck by lightning in the Netherlands every year

→ One in five Dutchmen over the age of 18 smokes

→ There are 417,000 unoccupied houses in the Netherlands

→ There are 22 B61-nuclear weapons stored in the Netherlands

- → The Netherlands occupies approximately 0.008 percent of the Earth's surface
- → Around Easter, the Dutch eat 32 million eggs
- → The Dutch are the tallest people in the world, at 170 cm for women and 184 cm for men
- → Approximately 464 people pass away in the Netherlands per day
- → 44 million people speak Dutch
- → The total length of Dutch roadways is 132,397 km. That is four times the circumference of the Earth
- → Zeeland is the Netherlands' sunniest province
- → The Netherlands has 1,500 - 1,550 hours of sunshine a year
- → A glass of tap water costs, on average, 0.03 euros
- → Per year 30,000 birds are killed by windmills
- → Every year, more than a million vibrators are sold in the Netherlands
- → Every year, the Dutch throw away 110 million loaves of bread
- → The Netherlands has 2,360 kilometers of highway
- → There are 15 municipalities in the Netherlands in which you are not allowed to swear
- → The most common surname in the US is Smith; in the world, Chang; and in the Netherlands, De Jong
- → On January 1, 2021, the Netherlands had 174,000 fully electric cars, an increase of more than 67,000 (63 percent) compared to the year before. The number of plug-in hybrids went up by 9 percent to more than 99,000.

Windmill Park, North Sea

Dubious Factoids

→ The Dutch soft drugs policy is impossible to explain; you can sell it, but you can't produce it. This falls under the banner of 'toleration'

→ These past years, the Dutch have been asking themselves the burning question: "If we are not tolerant, but also not intolerant – then what *are* we?"

→ There are more men than women in the Netherlands

→ The air over the Netherlands is considered the most polluted in Europe

→ The Dutch police and intelligence services are world champion eavesdroppers

→ The Netherlands is the class's bad boy when it comes to sustainable energy in Europe

→ The Netherlands has the most expensive Royal Family in Europe

→ The Netherlands has 2.5 million managers

→ 80 eurocents of every euro earned in the Netherlands goes to the government

→ The Dutch give their politicians an overall score of 4.5

→ The Dutch are not quick to give compliments

→ The Dutch are quick to criticize, but cannot take criticism themselves

→ Srebrenica and the Dutch East Indies are unpopular subjects in Dutch politics

Some Statitics

→ The Dutch population is the happiest in Europe

→ The Dutch have more faith in their fellow human beings than those of any other European Member State

→ The Netherlands has among the fewest graduates in sciences in Europe

→ Two-thirds of all those between 15 and 75 have a job, particularly a part-time job

→ 1 in 7 Dutch citizens is of non-Western origin

→ In 2035, the Netherlands will have 19 million inhabitants; in 2022 it reached 17.7 million

→ 3.8 percent of the employees is on sick leave

→ 90 percent of the population has broadband Internet at home, though glass fiber is gaining in popularity

→ There are more than 7.5 million homes in the Netherlands. Half of them are in the Western part of the country

→ Wholesalers in cheese, eggs and milk have an annual turnover of 13 billion euros

→ Health and welfare expenses amount to almost 100 billion euros, annually

→ The average value of a home is 400,000 euros

→ There are 3.7 million heads of cattle in the Netherlands

→ More than 100 farms cultivate wine grapes

→ The total mortgage debt in this country is approximately 765 billion euros

→ The Netherlands has 350 thousand hectares of woods, 10 percent of its total surface of 33,948 km²

→ The government deficit is 57.7 percent of the GPD (Gross Domestic Product)

→ The government debt amounts to 363 billion euros

→ Before Corona more than 71 million passengers passed through the Dutch airports

→ 49 percent of the Dutch population considers itself to be religious or adheres to a particular life philosophy

→ Dutch hotels accommodate 11 million foreign guests per year

→ The libraries lend out almost 75 million books a year

- → The Netherlands has 2,100 camping grounds
- → The Netherlands has more than 6.2 thousand kilometers of waterways
- → The Netherlands has 8.9 million cars and more than 1.3 million mopeds
- → 1990-2022: The emission of greenhouse gases in the Netherlands was reduced by 23.9%. This is below the Urgenda goal of at least 25 percent
- → The Netherlands' North Sea coastline is longer (642 km) than its border with either Belgium (407 km) or Germany (556 km)
- → About 60 percent of the population lives below sea level
- → The highest point is 321 (Limburg), the lowest 6.76 meters below sea level. It is in the northeast of Rotterdam
- → Head of State: King Willem-Alexander, Queen: Máxima
- → Type of state: constitutional monarchy
- → Seat of government: The Hague
- → Capital: Amsterdam
- → Number of households: 8 million
- → Average life expectancy men born now: 80 years, women: 83 years
- → Countries of origin of asylum-seekers: mostly Syria and Eritrea – though, in 2022, their numbers were far exceeded by Ukrainian asylum-seekers
- → Most important trade partner: Germany
- → Average income: 38,000 euros gross
- → Cost for employee per hour: NL 34.72 euros, Bulgaria 3.50 euros

Holland or
the Netherlands?

Now there's a good question: why is this country sometimes referred to as Holland and sometimes as the Netherlands? The official name of the country you have come to live in is the Netherlands, or 'Low Lands'; a country where 60 percent of the people live below sea level.

Then why is this country so often referred to as Holland? The answer to this question lies in its history. A few centuries ago, the province of Holland (which included today's North and South Holland provinces) was economically the strongest of all the Dutch provinces, and the one from which virtually all foreign trade originated. Most of the Dutchmen that foreign traders dealt with were Hollanders, literally from Holland. Hence, when talking about the Netherlands, this became the accepted way of referring to the country and its people. Over the years, both names have come to be accepted, although the official name, of course, remains the Netherlands.

Sensitivity

Though it is generally accepted that the Netherlands is referred to as Holland, those who are not from the provinces of North or South Holland do not like to be referred to as Hollanders, or to have their language referred to as *Hollands*. The other Dutch provinces are: Friesland, Groningen, Drenthe, Limburg, Utrecht, Gelderland, Overijssel, Noord-Brabant, Zeeland and Flevoland (the latter came into existence only 28 years ago and consists entirely of reclaimed land).

Randstad

Nowadays, it is of course – long since – no longer the case that the Holland provinces are the most advanced, though most businesses are still located in the provinces of North and South Holland and Utrecht – an area that is commonly referred to as the Randstad. The rest of the Netherlands is just as well-developed

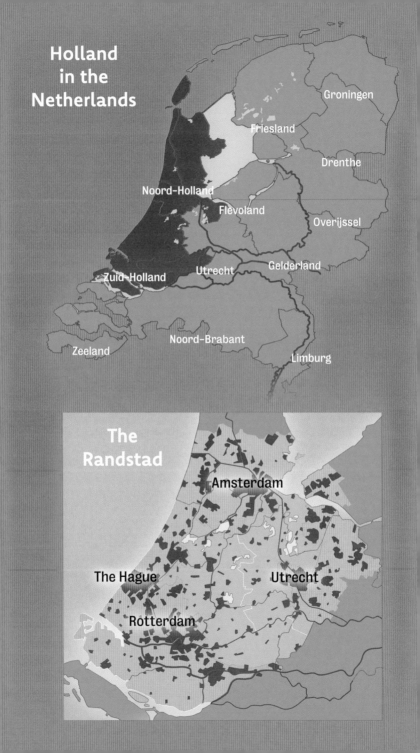

Holland
in the
Netherlands

Groningen

Friesland

Drenthe

Noord-Holland

Flevoland

Overijssel

Zuid-Holland

Utrecht

Gelderland

Zeeland

Noord-Brabant

Limburg

The
Randstad

Amsterdam

The Hague

Utrecht

Rotterdam

and houses many international businesses and expatriates, and the infrastructure (road, rail, water and telephone) is excellent, all across the country.

Official Name Change

On January 1, 2020, the country officially changed all official references to itself to 'the Netherlands'. Holland is considered merely a nickname and not official enough for Song Festivals or Olympics.

Things the Dutch Invented

1550 Orange-Colored Carrot Carrots used to come in all sort or colors; brown, purple, black, yellow and red. The Dutch cross-bred red and yellow carrots to come up with the orange color.

1574 National Anthem *Wilhelmus van Nassouwe* is the oldest national anthem in the world.

1606 Stock Exchange The Amsterdam stock exchange was the first of its kind in the world, trading in shares from the Dutch East India Company (VOC), which was also the world's first multinational corporation. When politicians today bemoan the lack of drive in the Netherlands, they call for a return to the VOC spirit.

1608 Telescope Dutchman Hans Lippershey failed to receive a patent for his invention but a copy of the design was used by Galileo Galilei. So ya boo sucks to Galileo. The Dutch can claim it.

1620 Submarine Cornelius Drebbel was the inventor of the first navigable submarine while working for the royal navy. Amazingly, his third prototype could carry 16 passengers and travelled under water from Westminster to Greenwich during a demonstration for Britain's King James 1.

1670s Microscope Anton van Leeuwenhoek became the first man to make and use a real microscope.

1672 Fire Hose Talented landscape painter Jan van der Heyden, and his brother Nicolaes, invented the first fire hose and was later put in charge of Amsterdam's firefighting department.

1828 Chocolate Bar Amsterdam chemist Casparus van Houten Sr. patented an inexpensive method for pressing the fat from roasted cocoa beans and creating a solid mass that could be pulverized into cocoa powder. This powder became the basis for chocolate products today.

1903 Electrocardiograph (ECG) Willem Einthoven was awarded a Nobel Prize for his invention.

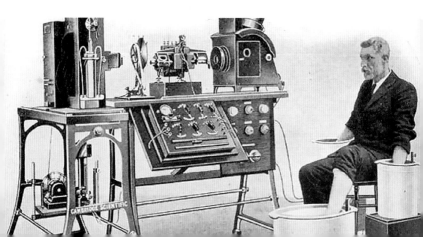

1903 Four-Wheel Drive with Internal Combustion Engine In 1903, the Dutch car manufacturer Spyker introduced the first four-wheel drive car with an internal combustion engine, the Spyker 60 HP. A revived Spyker Cars still makes luxury cars today. It also bought Saab which then went bankrupt.

Note: The Dutch think they invented printing but they didn't

1943 Artificial Kidney The first artificial kidney was developed by Willem Johan Kolf.

1958 Speed Camera Dutch company Gatsometer, founded by the 1950s rally driver Maurice Gatsonides, invented the first speed camera so that Gatsonides could monitor his speed around the corners of a race track. Perhaps not an invention to be proud of.

1979 Compact disc After the compact cassette in 1962, Philips together with Sony came up with the compact disc. Both now defunct of course.

1994 Bluetooth Jaap Haartsen invented the wireless communication system Bluetooth.

2005 Stormproof Umbrella Gerwin Hoogendoorn became frustrated and invented the stormproof umbrella.

2021 First fully solar-powered car Based on technology developed by ECN part of TNO.

World Heritage Sites

The Netherlands has ten UNESCO World Heritage sites, each of which represents a unique aspect of the Dutch history. In the near future, this list will be expanded upon.

Van Nelle Factory 2014

The Van Nelle factory was the tenth item to be added to the Dutch UNESCO World Heritage List. This is sure to be music to the ears of those who fought to avoid its destruction towards the end of the '90s of the previous century. Back in 1923, the then-director of Van Nelle ordered the construction of a 'hyper-modern' factory, which would provide space, light and air for the employees. The factory opened in 1931 and during the next 60 years produced tea, tobacco, coffee, instant pudding and chewing gum. Then, in 1995, production stopped, but luckily a group of investors came along and, in the mid-2000s, its doors opened again and it became a popular location for events and offices.

Van Nelle Factory, Rotterdam

Amsterdam Ring of Canals 2010

The Amsterdam Ring of Canals – 14 kilometers long and encompassing 80 bridges – is an urban planning, water management and architectural masterpiece. It was constructed around the 17th century – the Golden Age – and accompanied by the construction of narrow merchant's houses. Most of these houses had several stories and were where the merchants both lived and worked. At first, the houses varied little from each other, with the exception perhaps of their façades – with their stepped, neck and clock gables. Later came the construction of double canal houses and so-called manor houses, though this was reserved, of course, for the very wealthy. The latter houses have now acquired the name 'city palaces' and you can find them in the well-known *Gouden Bocht* (Golden Bend) of the Herengracht.

Willemstad Curaçao 1997

The inner city of Willemstad has been on the UNESCO World Heritage list since 1997 and is often referred to as the 'Amsterdam of the western hemisphere'. Here you will find a lot of authentic Dutch architecture, as well as street names that will remind you of the city's Dutch heritage, such as the Heerenstraat, Prinsenstraat and Breedestraat. Yet, the city's architecture is not all Dutch; it also has Portuguese influences and is, in fact, a colorful mix of styles. All in all, the typical Caribbean colors have become predominant.

Willemstad Curaçao

Droogmakerij De Beemster 1999

This particular World Heritage site is an entire municipality – with its beautiful, historic church and several museums, as well as authentic cheese-cover farmhouses, all surrounded by the typical North-Holland landscape. The best way to explore the town is on foot or by bicycle, following the route that takes you along the museums and the farmhouses – with the occasional place to stop and take a well-deserved rest.

Kinderdijk–Elshout Windmills 1997

There is no better place in the world to admire the development of water management than in Kinderdijk. Which is exactly why this site was added to the UNESCO World Heritage list. It encompasses a large polder area with storage basins, dikes, pumping stations and mills. It is *the* place to discover how the Dutch succeeded in laying dry and protecting the land.

Schokland 1995

Schokland was the first Dutch monument to be placed on the UNESCO list. Also here you can admire how the fate of the Dutch people is intermingled with that of the country's water. Initially, the island was located in what was then known as the Zuiderzee (now IJsselmeer) and its inhabitants were forced to watch, helplessly, as the wild sea claimed their land. It has since become an elongated strip of land that lies slightly higher than the surrounding polder and that houses several points of interest, including its church, lighthouse keeper's house, and the stones that were deposited there during the Ice Age – as well as other national monuments, archeological dike systems, mounds, and prehistoric sites.

Wadden Sea 2009

Whereas the Dutch and German portion made it onto the UNESCO list in 2009, the Danish part of the Wadden Sea was added in 2014. The three countries aim to work together to protect this area's natural habitat, which is the world's largest system of island, sand and mudflat plates – to a total of approximately 11,500 square kilometers, bringing it in a league with the Great Barrier Reef and the Grand Canyon!

The windmills of Kinderdijk

Wadden Sea

Rietveld Schröder House 2000

From 1923-1924, Gerrit Rietveld worked on the Rietveld Schröder House, whereby he was influenced by the art movement called 'De Stijl' ('The Style', or neoplasticism). He developed it in close collaboration with his client Truus Schröder-Schräder, who wanted it to be a place that was 'free from association' – for instance, the living room is not on the ground floor – which gave Mrs. Schröder a greater sense of freedom. After her death, the Centraal Museum took over its management and arranges exhibitions there, including a permanent exhibition containing some of Rietveld's pieces of furniture.

Ir. D.F. Wouda Pumping Station 1998

During the early 1900s, Friesland was besieged by water problems and in 1913 the decision was made to construct a pumping station near Lemmer. This was carried out by Ir. Dirk Frederik Wouda, head engineer of the Provincial section of the former Ministry of Transport, Public Works and Water Management. The pumping station is operational to this day and is yet another symbol of the Dutch people's daily struggle with water.

Defense Line of Amsterdam 1996

The Defense Line of Amsterdam is made up of 46 forts and batteries, as well as a tremendous amount of sluices and dikes – creating, all in all, a defense line of 200 kilometers. The aim was to protect Amsterdam against both water and invaders and it took approximately 40 years to create. It was finished just before the start of the First World War, though no battles ever took place here after its construction. It is open for visitors in many parts and is also a great place for hiking and cycling.

Colonies of Benevolence 2021

This site, which is made up of three locations – two in the Netherlands and one in Belgium – represents an experiment in social reform, focused on establishing agricultural colonies in remote locations to help combat poverty. The locations – Frederiksoord-Wilhelminaoord and Veenhuizen in the Netherlands, and Wortel in Belgium – were built in the early 19th century.

Veenhuizen has dormitory structures and centralized farms for orphans, beggars and vagrants who worked under the supervision of guards; Frederiksoord-Wilhelminaoord has small farms for families; and Wortel was first built for families and later became home to beggars and vagrants. Each component part has a distinctive spatial design and includes churches, farm houses, homes and communal buildings.

Frontiers of the Roman Empire
The Lower German Limes 2021

The Frontiers of the Roman Empire is a series of World Heritage sites located in seven countries, including Morocco, Slovakia and Ireland. The part that runs through the Netherlands follows the left bank of the Lower Rhine River the Rhenish Massif in Germany to the North Sea coast in the Netherlands. The archaeological remains include a fleet base, temporary camps, towers, fortresses and forts, as well as towns, an amphitheater, a palace and cemeteries. Almost all of the archaeological remains are buried underground.

The Dutch Culture

Core Values in Dutch Society

The core values in Dutch society are: freedom, equality and solidarity.

→ The Netherlands is a **democracy**. Its inhabitants have a say in who runs the country. It is also a **constitutional state**. Everyone has the same rights and must adhere to the same rules. Also the government.

→ Everyone is responsible for their own **sustenance**. If they are unable to do this – for whichever reason – there is a social safety net.

→ In order to succeed in the Netherlands you must learn Dutch. Which is why there is an assimilation course and obligation to attend this course.

→ Everyone has a right to **medical care**: to this purpose, everyone must take out medical insurance. This insurance will cover most of your medical expenses.

→ Children between the ages of 5 and 16 **must go to school**. If they have not graduated earlier, they must continue until the age of 18. (There are three types of high school here, from which you graduate at either age 16, 17 or 18 – provided you complete every year on schedule).

→ Everyone must pay **taxes**. The more you earn, the more you pay. The Dutch authorities use this tax money to pay for things that are in everyone's interest – such as roads, medical care, education and safety.

→ Dutch society – based on humanistic and Judeo-Christian traditions – is **open**. People are free to say what they think. No one is obligated to live according to any particular philosophy. Discrimination is punishable by law.

→ People of different **religious backgrounds** can live together safely here. No one may be made to feel threatened or unsafe because of their religion. You are free to demonstrate your beliefs through jewelry containing religious symbols, headscarves or yarmulkes. Some professions require uniform clothing, such as the army, the police or the courts.

→ Everyone is free to choose their own **lifestyle**. It's up to you what type of music you listen to, what type of clothes you wear, what type of work you do, which newspaper you read and what you eat. You can marry whomever you want and declare whichever sexuality you wish. There is of course a limit to all this freedom: you have to be considerate of other people and you may not incite violence.

→ The right to **self-determination** means that you can decide what you do with your body. No one may hurt you or even touch you if you don't want this. Even a doctor can only examine you with your permission. The law contains exceptions to this rule, such as in the case of police checks. The right to self-determination includes abortion and euthanasia.

→ All people are **equal** – not the same, for everyone is different – but deserving of equal treatment, be they man or woman, gay or 'straight', young or old, and born in the Netherlands or in another country.

→ **Solidarity** means that we take each other into account and that we know that others will do the same for us. The Netherlands is one of the richest countries in the world. But the government cannot be expected to do everything. Which is why it is important that people help each other. Many people here do volunteer work. For instance, in a sports club, or at schools. Others take care of someone at home, including offering to share their home with refugees for a while.

Through Other Eyes

Many Spaniards are of the opinion that the Netherlands smells of grass, trees and fallen leaves. The Turks think the Dutch should wash their butts and not wipe them. What do other people think of the Dutch?

→ The **Belgians**, our southern neighbors, are of the opinion that the Dutch are loud, hyperactive, immodest, and insensitive to hierarchy and authority. And they do not appreciate the 'Orange Madness' that accompanies soccer or skating. They are more positive about their neighbors when it comes to their tolerance, frugality, soberness, and assertiveness, as well as their love for the Royal Family, and their willingness to work hard. And they see the Dutch as entrepreneurial.

→ The **Spaniards** do not like the fact that you have to get out your agenda to make an appointment. They feel the Dutch neglect their elderly and they are not huge fans of the lunch sandwich. And they notice the stinginess. They are more appreciative, however, of the tolerance, generosity and thoughtfulness of the Dutch as well as of their well-organized roads and train stations...

→ The **French** do not appreciate Dutch food at all; the tomatoes are vile and their cheese has the texture of plastic. They also do not approve of the Dutch policy on soft drugs. They think the Dutch language is odd with all those guttural sounds and

they find the Dutch miserly. They become more enthusiastic when they discuss the Dutch arts and culture, their multilingualism, their straightforwardness, the flatness of the country, and its order and cleanliness.

→ The **English** really do not like the (rude) directness of the Dutch. However, they are more focused on the positive side: the easy-goingness of the Dutch, their relaxedness, multilingualism, beautiful women, sincerity, honesty and the relative lack of social classes.

Canal Gay Parade, Amsterdam

→ The **Hungarians** have no complaints. To them, the Netherlands is a wealthy nation with rich people, excellent roads and beautiful gardens.

→ The other neighbors, the **Germans**, are not quite as positive as their Hungarian friends. When asked, they come up with terms such as: loud, arrogant, pushy, stingy, drug users, with messy streets, chaotic roads and bad food in the restaurants. On the other hand, they find the Dutch entrepreneurial, welcoming, environmentally engaged, crazy about symmetry, and informal in the workplace, while the Germans enjoy coming here on short vacations, particularly to the Dutch coast.

→ Okay, let's take a look at a few other continents: **North America**. Negative, according to them: the use of weed, wooden shoes, mayonnaise on fries, nose-picking, lousy customer service and traffic jams.
Positive: easygoing/relaxed, welcoming, multilingual, tolerant, progressive, 'cute', tall and blond, good cheeses, creative, level-headed, direct, weather discussers, generally healthy, good company, while the country is green, full of flowers, flat, with short distances and few debts.

→ The **Russians** are the least enthusiastic about the Netherlands. On the positive side is the tolerance, but other than that – to them – the Netherlands is simply part of Germany: bad-mannered, fat inhabitants who eat like pigs and are stingy, loud, arrogant, boring, excessive smokers, wild about anything that's free and lacking in parenting skills. Interestingly, this is exactly how Dutch tourists describe the Russian tourists they come across abroad…

→ The **Japanese** – who in this case represent Asia – are of the opinion that the Dutch are rude, uncouth, egocentric, spoiled, undiplomatic and aggressive. On the other hand, they also see the Dutch as assertive, independent, creative and full of initiative.

Let's just say, wherever you're from, you're bound to be hit by at least a smidgen of culture shock.

Cultural Mistakes You Will Make

There are some things you cannot learn from integration courses, as a consequence of which there are a few glaring mistakes you just have to make to confirm that you are a true foreigner in the Netherlands. Here are a few that we have all been guilty of.

→ **You'll be late** Even one minute late is considered rude by Dutch standards. Traffic, getting lost, delays at work, difficulty finding parking, and every other excuse considered acceptable by all other nationalities will not earn you forgiveness. Though you can try to blame it on train delay. And curse the rudeness of NS to have made you late.

→ **You fail to make an appointment** Want grab coffee with your neighbor? Break out your calendar and schedule it 4-6 weeks in advance. Whatever you do, don't just drop by.

→ **You will forget flowers** If invited over to a Dutch person's home, you will be expected to bring a gift.
While some more open-minded folks will welcome a bottle of wine or chocolates, it's more common to bring flowers. And not flowers from Albert Heijn either.
But wait... Don't go getting a guy flowers, bring beer instead.

→ **You will not offer your colleagues coffee or tea** If you want grab a coffee during the work day, you better check with your entire office first, including janitorial staff and people on the night shift. Call them if necessary. You will be expected to bring back 14 different orders, because everyone in the office will say yes.

→ **You will decline something without saying thanks** If you do, god forbid, turn down your colleague's offer of coffee or tea, be sure to say "No, thank you" or "Nee, Bedankt". Even when declining the receipt at the grocery store, you better include that "thanks". Otherwise, you might as well spit on their shoes.

- → **You will not offer your guests tea or coffee** If anyone comes over to your house for any reason, you better be prepared to offer coffee, tea, and some type of biscuit. It doesn't matter if it's the plumber who is there because your sink exploded, or your future mother-in-law: you will be considered rude for not offering.
- → **You will fail to bring birthday cake to the office** It is your birthday, but you are expected to give everyone else a present – in the form of a piece of cake or pie. You must arrange the cakes, usually *Vlaamse Vlaaien*, next to the coffee machine.
- → **You will fail to congratulate your colleague on her husband's birthday** You congratulate everyone not only on their own birthday, but on the birthday of anyone who is near and dear to them. Failing to do this is considered insensitive and un-interested.

Nine Things Non-Dutch Children Love About Living in Holland

→ **Pancakes** This is at the top of nearly everyone's list. Dutch *pannenkoeken*, or pancakes, preferably with syrup and icing sugar, possibly banana and chocolate sauce, bacon and apple, shawarma, grilled chicken... you name it, you can have it on a pancake.

→ **Bikes** From about the age of four, Dutch kids can be seen riding their own bicycles, without training wheels, around the neighborhood. Were they born this way? Non-Dutch kids are soon addicted to the freedom a bike allows and – thanks to the cycle paths – as a parent you feel relaxed that your off-spring are safe cycling to school or to friends' houses. Not that you will manage to force them into a bike helmet of course. And as soon as they turn 15, they will start muttering about wanting a scooter.

→ **Hagelslag and other things on bread** Chocolate sprinkles on your sandwiches – not difficult to see why kids like this, or why becoming a dentist is something you should encourage your children to aim for. *Hagelslag*, chocolate paste, *speculaas* cookies, and *muisjes* – all sweet and delicious on soft, white bread! As an expat mother, your house may be boycotted by your children's friends unless you have *hagelslag* in the cupboard.

→ **Schools** No uniforms and almost no homework! If your kids have gone to school in almost any other country other than the Netherlands, attending a Dutch school, once they have tackled the language, is going to be a breeze. The no uniform policy is particularly loved by teenage girls, who grab the opportunity to dress up and perfect their makeup before cycling off to chemistry class.

→ **Amusement Parks** The Dutch love them – one of the most famous rollercoaster makers in the world is a Dutch company.

Be prepared to hand over a large heap of cash and spend a lot of time waiting in queues... but Walibi, Efteling, Linnaeshof, Duinrell, Drievelt, Slagharen and Hellendoorn, among others, are waiting for you.

→ **Skating** Like with bikes, Dutch kids are forced onto skates as soon as they can walk, so your expat kids will probably have some catching up to do. But if there is a big freeze, there will be no holding them back. Outdoor skating also means great pics to post on Facebook for admiring friends and relations.

→ **Sports** Forget school sports – in the Netherlands it's all about club competitions, whereby six and seven-year-old fanatical football players and hockey stars will find themselves whisked off to matches all over the place. Hockey clubs, in particular, appeal to teenage girls because they get to dress up in short skirts and have attitude at the same time. And don't forget the parties. Lots of parties.

→ **Birthdays** The egalitarian Dutch custom of ensuring no one gets left out means your children will soon come to associate every birthday with a little gift, whether or not it is their own birthday. As a parent, you will be driven insane by having to come up with something clever and imaginative to eat which your child can hand out in class in his or her birthday.

→ **Vice** So this is the one they don't talk about – but expat teens are secretly thrilled at the extra layer of cool that living in the sex and drugs-riddled Netherlands gives them among their friends in other places. But parents don't need to worry. Dutch kids have one of the lowest teen pregnancy rates in the world and are much less likely to abuse drugs than their peers in other countries. The UN says so.

Twelve Clues to Understanding the Dutch Mentality

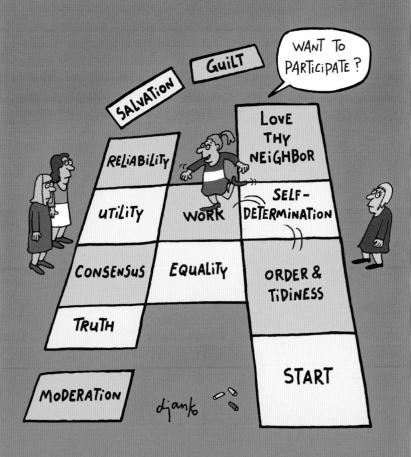

At first sight, the Dutch appear to be like many other normal Europeans. But those of you who have lived here longer and have worked with the Dutch, will have found dramatic differences. In short, it might be good to know a little more about the Dutch culture. In these paragraphs, you will find a short overview of the 12 principles or values that rule Dutch society, from politics, work, and school, to the most intimate parts of family life.

The first four values come straight from Christianity:

1 **Salvation**
Your sacrifices and efforts will be rewarded in the future

2 **Guilt**
You are responsible for the good and bad things that are the consequences of your acts

3 **Love thy neighbor**
You should be concerned about the welfare of others

4 **Truth**
You should always tell the bare facts

In the first place, the Dutch, just as other people who live in Christian cultures, are strongly oriented towards the future. Progress and innovation are important issues. Secondly, they are always worrying whether they did things right or wrong. The degree of personal responsibility is high. Thirdly, the Dutch feel greatly involved with people who have troubles, or who are suffering – whether close to home or on the other side of the world. This is evident from the country's extensive social security system and its high budget for developmental aid. Fourthly, the Dutch put a lot of stock in the objective truth and the bare facts. They find it more important to tell someone else exactly what they think than to be polite.

The next five values follow from Protestantism:

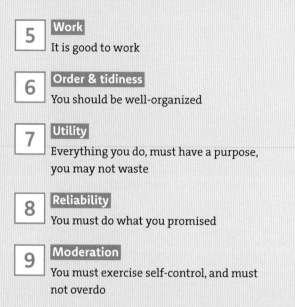

5 Work
It is good to work

6 Order & tidiness
You should be well-organized

7 Utility
Everything you do, must have a purpose,
you may not waste

8 Reliability
You must do what you promised

9 Moderation
You must exercise self-control, and must
not overdo

The Dutch think that it is better to work than to idly sit by. The higher they are on the corporate ladder, the harder they work. They appreciate an organized life that is dictated by the clock and their agenda, and think that a house should be neat and clean. The Netherlands is a relatively clean and well-organized country, in which a lot of big and little rules tell you how to behave. Also abroad, the Dutch are known for their tightness. One thing is certain; they hate waste; of money, time or anything else. Don't be surprised if they ask you what purpose your proposal serves. Couldn't it be done more efficiently, or perhaps effectively? The Dutch are very literal about their agreements and promises; if you agree to do something, then you must actually do it, or they will conclude that you are unreliable. In daily life, the Dutch hate extremes and exaggeration, they applaud self-restraint and frown upon expressing strong emotions. Only under certain conditions (a soccer match, carnival, at a disco), do they ever let it rip.

All this may sound pretty familiar to people from other Christian or Protestant countries. But the difficult part is still to come. The last three principles are typically Dutch and explain why certain things are done differently here or are found to be different than they are in the surrounding countries.

 ## Consensus
You should always try to compromise

The Dutch dislike conflict and aggression, and consistently strive for consensus and harmony, which they refer to affectionately as *gezelligheid*. They devote quite a bit of time to meetings and discussions, in order to make sure that all disagreements have been resolved. Instead of letting the democratic majority rule the minority, they prefer to find a solution that appeals to everyone; a compromise. A compromise that everyone will then stick to, for fear of conflict. This is often referred to as the *poldermodel*. Consequently, the Netherlands has a relatively peaceful, non-violent society, in which strikes end rather quickly in compromise and the police apply a de-escalating approach to handling skirmishes.

 ## Equality
You should not think that you are better than anyone else

In the Netherlands, all hierarchy and differences in social status are carefully smoothed over and disguised. It is painful to give direct instructions to someone who is under you, such as your cleaning lady. You can't just say: "Daisy, clean up the kitchen and the bathroom!" To the Dutch, this is a brusque order against which they rebel immediately. Instead, they formulate it as a polite question: "Would you perhaps be willing to do the kitchen and the bathroom today?" It sounds like a suggestion, but to the Dutch, this already feels like giving/receiving an order. The Dutch do not apply politeness towards superiors, but rather reverse politeness towards inferiors. You must, at all cost, avoid the impression that you think you might be superior to the other (even if you are a minister or have won the Nobel prize). It is perfectly easy to manage the Dutch, provided you treat them as equals and disguise every instruction as a friendly request.

The Dutch are allergic to people who toot their own horn; they expect modesty and if you fail to act like a 'normal' person, then you will be mowed down. You are not only not allowed to be openly proud of your achievements, the same applies to being proud of your country and your history. To many Dutch people, nationalism is a cardinal sin. This is not to say that the Dutch are not proud of their country; they just cannot say so openly.

12 Self-determination
I will decide what I do – not my father, boss or government

The Dutch find it more important that people be allowed to make their own choices, than to tell them what to do. Their motto is: everyone should decide for themselves what to do, as long as what they do doesn't interfere with my life. This is the basis for Dutch tolerance: it is not so much that they understand people who think differently, as that they are pragmatic; if you leave me alone, I will leave you alone. This explains why the Dutch tolerate the use of soft drugs, abortion and euthanasia. It does not so much mean that they 'do' it, but rather that they feel that whether or not someone else does, is their personal choice and none of anyone's business. This explains why so many different lifestyles can coexist in such a small country, from extravagant gay people who marry, to black-clad orthodox protestants who go to church three times every Sunday.

Children are not so much raised to respect their elders or general moral principles – but to think for themselves and speak for themselves. Dutch employees are expected to demonstrate a high degree of responsibility and initiative. Do take into account therefore that all Dutch people, be they young or old, have an opinion on everything and want to be heard. After which they will call a meeting, to reach a compromise!

Popular Finger Food

T op 10 yummy (at least, as far as the Dutch are concerned), typical Dutch finger food.

 1 Cubes of cheese or sausage with a piece of pickle or silver-skin onions on a toothpick that has a Dutch flag at the end

Probably the easiest-to-recognize finger food. Easy to prepare and festive-looking with its little flag.

2 Bitterballen (deep-fried meat ragout, coated in bread crumbs)

Another classic – and Dutcher than Dutch. Don't forget to serve them with mustard; an essential ingredient for creating that authentic '*bitterbal*-experience'.

3 Dutch meat balls

These are very popular here. Though they are easy to prepare, no two are the same and some families strictly guard their secret recipe over generations.

4 Deviled eggs

Another party favorite. They look complicated, but are easy to make. Hard-boil eggs, peel them, cut them in half, remove the egg yolk. Mix the yolk with grated cheese, sour cream, chives, garlic, ginger syrup, pepper and salt. Scoop back into the halves of egg white and sprinkle with ground paprika.

5 Toast with herring, eel and salmon

Make toast (or use crackers) and cover with either herring, eel or salmon. These go back centuries!

6 Toast with 'salad'

The modern-day version of toast with fish. In this case, you buy egg salad, tuna salad, crab salad, chicken curry salad... and serve it on toast (or crackers).

7 Rye bread with herring and onions

Not hard to prepare: take a slice of rye bread, place herring on top, sprinkle with chopped onion and voilà.

8 Mini cheese soufflés

Something you would be hard put to find outside the Netherlands. Serve with mayonnaise, curry sauce or chili sauce.

9 Potato salad

An excellent dish to serve along with the previous finger foods. You usually place it on the table so that people can serve themselves. Eaten with a fork.

10 French bread (with garlic butter)

Another side dish to accompany the finger foods. You can cut it in little round slices and place these on the table, in a basket. Or you can place it on a cutting board with a knife and let your guests do their own slicing. Place a generous dish of garlic butter next to it.

Typical Dutch Festivities

Carnival

Carnival, the Dutch either love it or hate it. Those who live *beneden de rivieren* (below the rivers, in other words in Noord-Brabant or Limburg) love it and celebrate it with a passion. Virtually all businesses close (except cafés and restaurants of course) in a three-day celebration of life, spring, beer and friendship. In the provinces *boven de rivieren* (above the rivers) the general attitude towards carnival is one of aloofness – adding to their reputation among the Southerners as a dour and 'un-fun' people – a gray dividing line that, some would say, smacks of a still Protestant-based north and a predominantly Catholic south.

People get dressed up and go from café to café, singing songs, participating in parades and consuming large quantities of beer. There is no need to be afraid of this being a local festivity at which strangers are not accepted: strangers are welcome, and it is a great way to meet new people. Breda, Maastricht and 's Hertogenbosch are three of the major venues.

Carnival Breda

April 27: King's (Birth)Day

Although not necessarily known to be royalists, the Dutch are extremely fond of their Royal Family. Throughout history, the Dutch Royal Family has been very popular and the Family's birthdays have been celebrated with enthusiasm.

You can celebrate the King's birthday either by visiting the town or city the King visits on this day – and witness traditional entertainment and games – or you can visit some of the bigger cities. Amsterdam, in particular, goes all out on this day, with a *vrijmarkt*, a free market that fills the streets in the center of Amsterdam with stands run by people age 5 – 105, selling anything and everything. People from all across the world come to Amsterdam. Another option is to visit the traditional *koningsmarkt* (King's Market) of your own town, where the locals sell just about anything for a song, a great opportunity for bargain hunters and antique buffs – but be there early for the best values (6 A.M.)!

Commemorating the Dead: May 4th

More a day of national significance than of festivity, May 4th is initially the day on which the Dutch remember the victims of the Second World War: soldiers, people in the Resistance and those who died in the concentration camps in Europe as well as in Indonesia. Since 1961, the commemoration has been expanded to include all war victims in the years since the Second World War. Between 8 P.M. and 8:02 P.M., a two-minute silence is observed nationally. People stop whatever they are doing (often pulling their cars over to the side of the road) to remember those who were victims of a war. Even local radio and television broadcasts are halted. In many municipalities, people come together for short ceremonies, particularly in The Hague, on the Waalsdorpervlakte, and in Amsterdam, on the Dam Square. Flags are hung half-mast throughout the country.

Liberation Day: May 5th

Following the sober day of May 4th, the Dutch celebrate their total liberation from the occupying forces in 1945 (some parts of the Netherlands had been liberated in November 1944) on Liberation Day, May 5th. This day is not celebrated as extensively as it used to be: some businesses and most government offices close (in keeping with the collective labor agreement), but most do not. However, there is always some celebration going on somewhere, while movies and documentaries about this period on TV provide you with the opportunity to learn a little bit about (recent) Dutch history if you want.

Trick or Treats – Sint Maarten

Increasingly, the trick or treats day of November 11 is being reintroduced. On this day, children (often accompanied by parents) come by your door, carrying lanterns and singing songs such as '*Sint Maarten, Sint Maarten, de koeien hebben staarten, de meisjes hebben rokjes aan, daar komt Sint Martinus aan*' (St. Martin, St. Martin, the cows have tails, the girls wear skirts, there comes St. Martin – who *knows* what the one has to do with the other). This day is a 'treats'-day – no tricks – the treats being anything from tangerines to cookies to candy. The children do not get dressed up for this occasion, either; it is a simple – though friendly and *gezellige* – neighborhood event. In some cities, due to the exposure to other cultures, rather than with Sint Maarten on November 11, children *do* dress up and go trick or treating on October 31, Halloween.

Sinterklaas

December 5th is St. Nicholas's birthday when, according to legend, this 4th-century Saint gave gifts of gold to three poor girls for their dowries (children still receive chocolate coins around this time). As Sinterklaas is considered the patron saint of children, he brings them gifts that are surreptitiously dropped off in a sack on the doorstep of the Dutch households – where children live – on December 5th. (Usually, a neighbor is involved in this process: the parents bring them the sack sometime during the day and they promise to drop it on the doorstep and bang on the door. This is the cue for the children to yell 'Sinterklaas!' and run to the door, in hopes of catching the retreating form of Sinterklaas or Zwarte Piet. Instead, they find the sack of gifts and completely fail to notice the happy neighbor, hidden around the corner, having made their escape just in time.)

Somewhere mid-November, Sinterklaas makes his official entry into the Netherlands, arriving on his steamboat from Spain, accompanied by his helpers, the Pieten. Between his arrival and December 5, you can find him all across the country, visiting businesses, schools and people's homes, bringing candies, cookies and gifts. He and his helpers may also decide to pay a kid's home a surprise visit at night. In order to limit the excitement,

parents usually compromise to having him visit twice a week, say on Tuesday night and Saturday night, in order not to be dragged out of bed at 6 o'clock *every* morning to see if there are any surprises.

Sinterklaas's birthday is not only a holiday for children; grown-ups like to participate in the fun by means of a gift (serious, silly or, often, homemade, called a *surprise*) with an accompanying poem that summarizes the receiver's past year, intermingled with surprising habits and silly mistakes – often in a slightly ridiculing tone. (Bear in mind that the Dutch love to tease and the more fun they make of you, the more they like you, although it has been known to happen that the unsuspecting non-Dutch receiver of such a lovingly and amusingly composed poem has rushed out of the room in tears.)

Sinterklaas's helpers – the Pieten – used to go by the name of 'Zwarte Piet' (Black Pete), and had deeply blackened faces, while they wore curly black wigs, golden hoops in their ears and colorful clothing. This has given rise to enough controversy in recent years that the adjective 'zwart' has been replaced by 'roet' (soot) and 'kleur' (color – *not* colored). The soot Piets have smears of soot on their faces and clothing from going up and down the chimneys to deposit presents, and the color Piets come in all colors of the rainbow. This change has been gradual, from 'no way' to 'okay' and the Dutch are getting used to this new version – in fact, many simply do not tolerate any reference to the old version at all.

Christmas

Christmas itself is normally reserved for religious observances and family get-togethers – with some gifts, perhaps, for the kids. The Dutch do not celebrate Christmas Eve – though they do attend church services in the evening – instead they have First and Second Christmas Day. Which lend themselves excellently for visiting first one set of in-laws, and then the next on the next day.

Dutch National Holidays and Main Festivities

January 1	New Year's Day
February 14	Valentine's Day
February/March	Carnival
March/April	Good Friday
March/April	*Pasen* – Easter Sunday and Monday
April 27	*Koningsdag* – King's (Birth)day
May 4	*Dodenherdenking* (Commemoration of the Dead)
May 5	*Bevrijdingsdag* (Liberation Day)
May	*Hemelvaartsdag* (Ascension Day)
May, 2nd Sunday	Mother's Day
May/June	*Pinksteren* (Whit Sunday) and *Tweede Pinksterdag* Monday (Whit Monday)
June, 3rd Sunday	Father's Day
September, 3rd Tuesday	*Prinsjesdag* (Opening of Parliament)
October 4	*Dierendag* (International Animal Day)
November 11	St. Maarten
December 5	Sinterklaas
December 25 and 26	First and Second Christmas Day
December 31	New Year's Eve

Thiemepark, Nijmegen

The Steamier Side
of Society

High on the to-do list of every visitor to the Netherlands, right up there with the famed museums, is a walk on the wild side of seemingly sedate Dutch society: a tour of the red-light district in Amsterdam. The *wallen* ('the walls'), as that part of town is known, lives up to its billing. Everything you expect is there. Teeming crowds juxtaposing businessmen and tourists; prostitutes publicly ensconced in the windows of the numerous business establishments; the quote-unquote coffee shops that sell everything from Thai stick to space cakes – coffee definitely not being the specialty of the house.

Point of View

After soaking in the sights for a few minutes, you may realize that the only thing that makes the goings-on into a spectacle is your point of view. Having spent some time in the Netherlands, you probably aren't surprised that everything is well-organized (the Dutch police even have an English-language how-to guide to help tourists safely explore the steamier side of the city); but you probably did not expect it to be 'dead normal', as the Dutch say. The only difference between the streets of the red-light district and other shopping districts in the city is the merchandise. While there are prostitutes and drugs in every large city, Dutch or otherwise, in the Netherlands both businesses are given an air of legitimacy that exceeds that found in most other countries. Like so many other visitors, you marvel at the tolerant Dutch in action.

Clichés

Noting that the Dutch are tolerant, however, is not exactly a radical discovery. Social experiments in the Netherlands are sufficiently renowned that such comments are almost clichés. But there is more to this than just being open-minded. Most visitors are shocked when they learn that until recently prostitution was illegal and that the possession or sale of recreational drugs remains against the law. After one day in Amsterdam, it is hard to believe that any of this ever was a criminal offense – which, in a sense, is correct: even when illegal, these activities occurred and thrived with the tacit approval of the local community and the Dutch government.

Tolerance vs. Acceptance

Don't confuse Dutch realism with loose mores. As individuals, most are principled; a fair number are very religious. When asked, the overwhelming majority indicates that they don't use drugs or prostitutes, and the statistics bear this out. Remarkably, the Dutch make a distinction between their values and what they expect from others. While there is general agreement that recreational drugs and prostitution are social evils, there is also a strong consensus that they are going to occur whether they are illegal or not and that prosecution often results in social ails worse than the original malady. Thus, it is better to mitigate the negative aspects of these activities with regulation (what could be more Dutch than that?) than to drive them underground through futile attempts at eradication. That these vices were or are still technically illegal is mostly a reflection of the consensus-building that is implicit to Dutch public policy: it is one thing to passively accept certain activities as inevitable; it is another to actively endorse them. In short, there is a big difference between tolerance and acceptance.

A Work in Progress

Sounds great. But how well do these Dutch approaches work? The answer depends on your priorities. In the case of prostitution, the public-health accomplishments are impressive. Thanks to access to medical care and routine testing, the physical well-being of most prostitutes and their clients is significantly better in the Netherlands than in many other countries. Unfortunately, rules only protect those who are a part of the system, and even then, only those who are able to understand and use them. In particular, many of the prostitutes are thought to be illegal immigrants, including an unknown number who were coerced into the trade and work in de facto slavery. Due to fear of reprisals or deportation, it is less likely that foreign prostitutes will contact the authorities for help if they need it. Recent attempts to expand government control by legalizing brothels may have made things worse: the added expense has driven some activity underground. While such problems are not unique to the Netherlands, the abuse of these individuals, in spite of the existing rules and regulations, is, to say the least, extremely troubling to the Dutch.

Too Pragmatic?

All of this leads some to conclude that the Dutch are too pragmatic. The foreign press invariably carries stories that make you shake your head in wonder, such as the one about the Dutch parents who ran the coffee shop in their town: if their children were going to experiment with controlled substances, they felt better knowing who was selling them the drugs! Nonetheless, in spite of the occasional excesses and the remaining problems, rational social policies as well systematic and open education on sex, drugs as well as alcohol have successfully encouraged responsible behavior. As a consequence, most Dutch teenagers choose abstinence or practice safe sex, as evidenced by the low rates of sexually transmitted diseases, teen pregnancies and abortions. (Even dictionaries for Dutch tourists propagate the party line. When it comes to sex, the content is restricted to such useful phrases as 'Only with a condom' and 'Let's not take any chances'.) Furthermore, while most Dutch teenagers go through a period of exploration, where some experiment with drugs, most move on: teenage and adult drug usage rates are relatively low.

While it may not be politically or culturally feasible for other countries to adopt these policies or approaches, one cannot help but admire what the Dutch have accomplished.

Red Light District 'De Wallen', Amsterdam

Alcohol Use and Drugs

Sale of Liquor

Sale of Liquor

From the age of 18 onwards you may legally buy beer, wine and liquor. Alcoholic beverages can be bought in liquor stores and supermarkets – though supermarkets only sell beer, wine and alcoholic beverages with an alcohol percentage up to 12 to 13 percent.

Bartenders, liquor dealers and cashiers must ask youngsters who are buying alcohol from them to submit proof of their age, such as a passport, ID-card or driver's license. If any one of these cannot be supplied, they are not allowed to sell it to them.

Drinking and Driving

→ You may not drive if you are over the 0.5-blood alcohol level or, during the first five years after you have been issued a driver's license; 0.2

→ This latter limit also applies to drivers of mopeds and motorized bicycles until the age of 24

→ Driving under the influence is a criminal offense and applies to driving a car and riding a motorcycle, scooter, moped or bicycle

→ You risk a fine running from 300 euros to 1,100 euros (125 euros to 225 euros, if you are riding a moped or a scooter), depending on your blood alcohol level, plus a possible ban on driving of up to almost a year and possible incarceration

→ If you are caught driving under the influence of soft or hard drugs, you run the risk of three months of incarceration, having your driver's license suspended for five years, or a fine of up to 21,750 euros.

Coffee shops are not only found in the bigger cities: there are approximately 564 coffee shops, down from approximately 1,500 25 years ago, spread over 100-plus municipalities. So don't be surprised if your sleepy little village has one too.

Drug Use

For the record, trafficking in (importing or exporting), selling, producing and processing either hard or soft drugs are offenses in the Netherlands. The possession of soft drugs (up to 30 grams) or hard drugs (0.5 grams) for personal use is a summary, non-indictable offense. However, if you wish to buy soft drugs, the Netherlands is famous for its coffee shops...

Coffee Shops

A coffee shop can best be described as a café that does not sell alcoholic beverages (except in Amsterdam, where some do), but that does sell soft drugs. Low priority is given to the prosecution of coffee shop owners, provided they sell small quantities only and meet the following conditions:

→ no more than five grams per person are sold in any one transaction
→ the stock does not exceed 500 grams

Per day, the police close an average of 20 illegal cannabis farms. All in all, these plantations, what with enforcement, investigation, stolen electricity and fires, cost the government 447 million euros a year. It is estimated that 60,000 plantations generate an annual turnover of 4 billion euros and legalizing them would fill the state coffers with an additional 850 million euros, if they levied the equivalent of cigarette taxes, as well as 400 million euros if they levied VAT. However, this would not be beneficial for this country's relations with the United Nations, the European Union or the Schengen countries, as the Netherlands has agreed in several treaties that drugs will remain illegal.

- → no alcohol is served on the premises
- → no online sales or home deliveries are provided
- → no hard drugs are sold
- → the drugs are not advertised
- → the coffee shop does not cause any nuisance
- → no drugs are sold to persons under the age of 18, nor are minors admitted onto the premises.

Municipalities may set up extra rules, for instance regarding the proximity to schools. Agreements are made with the local police regarding routine checks and the mayor of a city has the authority to close coffee shops that do not meet these conditions.

Legal Gymnastics

The Dutch government has to perform legal gymnastics in order to make the sale of soft drugs in coffee shops possible. To make the existence of coffee shops possible, two terms have been introduced: *gedoogbeleid* (policy of tolerance) and *lage opsporingsbeleid* (policy of low investigational priority). The sale of soft drugs in coffee shops is tolerated and, provided the conditions are met, the culturing of soft drugs to be sold via coffee shops will not be prosecuted. The interesting question is: Why is this tolerated? The answer brings to light a specific desire that typifies Dutch society: the aim of this policy is to prevent users of soft drugs from becoming marginalized or being exposed to more harmful drugs.

Though shop owners may not charge VAT over their sales, they do owe income tax over their income; generating a pleasant calculated 400 million euros a year for the state coffers.

Drug Tourism

In an aim to quash drug tourism, if you want to buy drugs, you have to be a legal resident of the Netherlands. It is up to the coffee shop owner to verify this – which, if you think about it, is probably a lot to ask of them...

Museums

An overview of important, not-to-be missed museums in the Netherlands in order of top-number of visitors:

1 **Rijksmuseum** (Imperial Museum)
Dedicated to arts and history in Amsterdam. It is located on the Museum Square in the borough Amsterdam South, close to the Van Gogh Museum, the Stedelijk Museum Amsterdam, and the Concertgebouw. The main building was designed by Pierre Cuypers and first opened its doors in 1885. On April 13, 2013, after a ten-year renovation which cost 375 million euros, the main building was reopened by Queen Beatrix. In that year alone, it attracted 2,220,000 visitors. It now attracts approximately 3 million visitors a year, making it the the most visited museum in the Netherlands. On display are 7,000 objects of art and history, from a total collection of 1 million objects from the years 1200–2000, among which are masterpieces by Rembrandt, Frans Hals and Johannes Vermeer.

2 Van Gogh Museum

Dedicated to the works of Vincent van Gogh and his contemporaries and is also located on the Museum Square. It is located in buildings designed by Gerrit Rietveld and Kisho Kurokawa. The museum's collection is the largest collection of Van Gogh's paintings and drawings in the world. The museum welcomes an annual 1.7 million visitors.

3 Anne Frank House (Anne Frank Huis)

A biographical museum dedicated to Jewish wartime diarist Anne Frank. The building is located on a canal called the Prinsengracht, close to the Westerkerk, in central Amsterdam. During World War II, Anne Frank hid from Nazi persecution with her family and four other people in hidden rooms at the rear of this 17th-century canal house, known as the Secret Annex (Dutch: Achterhuis). Anne Frank did not survive the war, but in 1947 her wartime diary was published. In 1957, the Anne Frank Foundation was established to protect the property from developers who wanted to demolish the block. The museum preserves the hiding place, has a permanent exhibition on the life and times of Anne Frank, and has an exhibition space on all forms of persecution and discrimination. The museum attracts an annual 1.2 million visitors and was the 3rd most visited museum in the Netherlands.

Van Gogh Museum Amsterdam

4 Stedelijk Museum Amsterdam
(Municipal Museum Amsterdam)

Colloquially known as the Stedelijk, is a museum for modern art, contemporary art, and design and is located in Amsterdam. The 19th-century building was designed by Adriaan Willem Weissman and the 21st-century wing with the current entrance was designed by Benthem Crouwel Architects. It is located on the Museum Square. The collection comprises modern and contemporary art and design from the early 20th century up to the 21st century. It features artists such as Vincent van Gogh, Wassily Kandinsky, Ernst Ludwig Kirchner, Marc Chagall, Henri Matisse, Jackson Pollock, Karel Appel, Andy Warhol, Willem de Kooning, Marlene Dumas, Lucio Fontana, and Gilbert & George. Annually, the museum welcomes an estimated 675,000 visitors.

5 Science Center Nemo

A science center in Amsterdam. It is located at the Oosterdok in Amsterdam-Centrum. The museum has its origins in 1923, and, since 1997, is housed in a building designed by Renzo Piano. It contains five floors of hands-on science exhibitions and is the largest science center in the Netherlands. Annually, it attracts almost 600,000 visitors, which makes it the fifth most visited museum in the Netherlands.

6 Kunstmuseum Den Haag (Art Museum The Hague)

An art museum in The Hague. The museum, built 1931–1935, was designed by the Dutch architect H.P. Berlage. It is renowned for its large Mondriaan collection, the largest in the world. His last work, *Victory Boogie-Woogie*, is on display here. GEM (museum for contemporary art) and Fotomuseum Den Haag (The Hague museum for photography) are part of the Kunstmuseum, though not housed in the same building and with a separate entrance fee. The museum's collection of modern art includes works by international artists (Edgar Degas, Claude Monet, Pablo Picasso, Egon Schiele, Frank Stella, Henri Le Fauconnier and many others) and Dutch artists (Charlotte Dumas, Pyke Koch, Piet Mondriaan, Charley Toorop, Jan Toorop, Hans Wilschut and many others). Annually, it attracts almost 600,000 visitors.

7 Mauritshuis (Maurice House)

An art museum in The Hague. The museum houses the Royal Cabinet of Paintings which consists of 841 objects; mostly Dutch Golden Age paintings. The collections contain works by Johannes Vermeer, Rembrandt van Rijn, Jan Steen, Paulus Potter, Frans Hals, Jacob van Ruisdael, Hans Holbein the Younger, and others. Originally, the 17th-century building was the residence of count John Maurice of Nassau. It is now the property of the government of the Netherlands and is listed in the top 100 Dutch heritage sites. Annually, it attracts almost 500,000 visitors.

8 Nationaal Militair Museum
(National Military Museum)

Situated on the former air base at Soesterberg. It combines the collections of the former Military Aviation Museum in Soesterberg and Army Museum in Delft and its collection runs from arrows from the Stone Age, swords and harnesses from the Middle Ages, to items from the current weapons system of the Dutch army. There are airplanes, canons, and tanks, including seven different jet fighter planes in a 'dogfight', a Leopard 1V and 2 fighter tank, and an M270 Multiple Launch Rocket System (MLRS). A top piece of the collection is the V2, the rocket with which the Germans attacked the Allied Forces in Southern Netherlands, Belgium and England from Northern Netherlands. This was the first operational and steerable rocket. Annually, the museum attracts almost 500,000 visitors.

9 Nederlands Openluchtmuseum
(Netherlands Open Air Museum)

An open-air museum and park located near Arnhem with historic houses, farms and factories from different parts of the Netherlands. The Netherlands Open Air Museum focuses on the culture associated with the everyday lives of ordinary people. Annually, it attracts almost 450,000 visitors.

Hermitage Amsterdam

A branch museum of the Hermitage Museum of Saint Petersburg, Russia, and is located on the banks of the Amstel river in Amsterdam. The museum is located in the former Amstelhof, a classical-style building from 1681. It is currently the largest satellite of the Hermitage and annually attracts more than 400,000 visitors.

Other important museums include Boijmans (Rotterdam), Frans Hals (Haarlem), Kröller-Müller (Otterlo), Bonnefanten (Maastricht) and many, many more.

Websites
→ www.museumgidsnederland.nl/en
→ www.artcyclopedia.com/museums/art-museums-in-the-netherlands
→ www.holland.com/global/tourism/activities/arts-culture/museum.htm

The Dutch Language

Learning Dutch

Okay, if you're in one of the bigger cities in Holland, and you venture into the Dutch language, then – at the first trip or hint of an accent – your conversation partner/waiter/storeowner will probably switch to English. Which is probably a relief, but also makes it hard to ever learn the language.

This does not mean, however, that the Dutch are totally okay with your never learning the language – or that you can can get away with English all the time, particularly outside the big cities. The Dutch are very helpful and are proud of their command of the English language, but if, after three or so years, you still cannot order your *volkorenbrood* in Dutch, their font of sympathy might dry up.

Basically, it could be considered a sign of respect to learn the language of your host country, and, if you really want to integrate further, get to know the culture and develop local friendships, you have little choice *but* to learn the language – however daunting it may seem.

Why Should You Learn Dutch?

If you are the partner or spouse of an employee who has been placed in the Netherlands, you will have time on your hands and find yourself facing the need to navigate daily life in the Dutch language. Particularly if you are looking for a job here, too. Wherever you live, you feel more comfortable with your life if you can understand what's going on around you, what is listed in the job openings, what it says on the packages in the supermarket, and what that sign means by the bus stop/in the storefront/at the train station.

If have kids, they will probably pick up the language easily as they play with the kids in the streets, navigate Dutch children's TV, or attend school – if they are going to a Dutch one.

How Difficult Is Dutch?

Dutch is not an easy language for English speakers – we simply do not have the capacity for those throaty, guttural sounds on which Netherlandish children are weaned. Sentence structure is awkwardly reversed, and the Dutch love to glue words together into one seemingly endless hangman challenge. Words such as *ziektekostenverzekering* (health care insurance) or *projectontwikkelingsmaatschappijen* (meaning 'property development companies') leave you wondering where one syllable begins and the other ends.

If you have some knowledge of German, or perhaps Danish, stored in your brain, you might feel less challenged – but that is only because you've taken this hurdle into a Germanic language before! (Native speakers of these languages, of course, will be at the top of the class.)

The First Steps

You can follow an established course or take private lessons. Holland has a national network of language institutes that offer courses in Dutch to foreigners. These courses are generally referred to as NT2, *Nederlands als tweede taal* (Dutch as a second language). You can find one through your city hall or else by asking around or surfing the Internet. When you have found an institute, they may ask you what type of school you went to at home, what diplomas you have, whether you interact with a lot of Dutch people, whether you have time to go to a school and to do homework, etc. You might also be asked to take a placement exam to determine what level you should pursue. Depending on your specific needs, the institute may suggest an intensive course for quicker immersion.

TIP Dutch numbers require some mental gymnastics – '79' is expressed as 'nine and seventy', for example – so be prepared.

A Few Words of Advice

Let the person you're talking to know that you don't (or hardly) speak any Dutch Don't give in to the temptation to do it all in English, as you'll never learn Dutch that way. If you say *Ik wil Nederlands leren*, the Dutch will be more than happy to comply.

Do not be afraid to make mistakes Don't expect to speak Dutch as well as you do your native language – it will only make you insecure, and why demand so much of yourself? Fluency takes much time, and all that matters at first is basic communication.

Pick your moments It isn't always the right moment to insist on speaking Dutch. Be sure there isn't a long line of hurried and harried locals who 'want to get on with their lives' behind you.

Don't make it unnecessarily hard Keep your initial conversations simple.

Don't be afraid to admit you still don't know what they're saying Just say: "Sorry, I'm afraid I still don't get it. Could you repeat it in English, please?" They've just seen you try very hard to connect in their language, and they'll be more than willing to return the effort.

Absorb all day As you hear Dutch in your daily activities, pay attention to what others are saying and how they say it. Look up a word or two at the end of the day, and check out the Dutch subtitles on your favorite TV show. It's a great way to practice.

Which Dutch?

Not all Dutch people speak the same Dutch language. There is a standard language: *Algemeen Beschaafd Nederlands* (ABN), which translates into the somewhat pompous-sounding 'General Civilized Dutch'. It is what 'well-educated' Dutch people who live in the Randstad (the area comprising Amsterdam, The Hague, Rotterdam, Utrecht and everything in between) speak. This was once the old dialect of the District of Holland, the most powerful province – which is why *Hollands* became the most widespread dialect in the country.

The other regions in the Netherlands speak the same language, but the pronunciation can be quite different and hard to understand at first. Having mastered Dutch in The Hague will not prepare you at all for *Zeeuws*, *Twents*, *Gronings*, *Drents*, or *Brabants* – let alone *Limburgs* (spoken in Limburg), which to many doesn't even *sound* like Dutch, but more like German and Flemish, mixed into one. Also the people from the various cities all have their very distinct way of pronouncing the language. The Dutch can tell within a sentence whether someone is from The Hague, Amsterdam, Rotterdam or Utrecht.

In Friesland, a province in the northwest of Holland, aside from Dutch, they speak Frisian. Many of the words used are the same – but pronounced differently – but they also have a whole unique vocabulary. An interesting factoid to note is that Frisian is considered, historically, to be closer to the English language than Dutch is.

The End Result

If you are planning on staying here for a long time, learning Dutch will help you integrate. In fact, in our item on *Inburgering – Integrating into Dutch Society*, you will read that in many cases, you are obligated to learn the language if you plan on building a life here. How far you get will depend on whether or not you have the time, talent and inclination to master another language. If you decide to go for it, we wish you luck and fun! And don't forget, just about any foreign accent will give the Dutch language something extra to make it a little more palatable.

Essential Dutch Expressions

You may be learning Dutch, you may be ignoring the language altogether or you may be a fluent speaker. Here is a handy list of 10 Dutch expressions which everyone needs to know.

→ *Doe maar normaal dan doe je al gek genoeg*. Just behave normally; this is already crazy enough. Guess the translation says all.
→ *Heb ik wat van je aan?* When you look at a Dutch person fixedly they may ask you if they are wearing something of yours. This is not meant kindly so take care not to stare.

→ *Daarom* (pronounced: *derooom*). This means 'exactly' and is an expression of concurrence. However, it usually has nothing to do with what the other speaker has just said. It's either an excuse to take over the conversation or a ploy to mask the fact that you have been fast asleep for the last five minutes.

→ *Krijg toch de tering/kanker/typhus*. "Get TB/cancer/typhoid" – take your pick – is an example of the Dutch predilection for wishing nasty diseases on people. Sometimes followed by *achter je hart* (behind your heart).

→ *Ik zeg maar zo, ik zeg maar niks*. I'll just say I say nothing. Typical example of Dutch poldering: prudent, non-committal, on the fence.

→ *Dat kan niet*. It can't be done, impossible. Phrase familiar to expats faced with Dutch bureaucracy.

→ *Doe effe normaal.* Behave. Made famous by Geert Wilders who said it to the prime minister in parliament, this expression is indicative of the Dutch wish to appear 'normal' and not stand out.

→ *Doe je dat (bij je moeder) thuis ook?* Do you do that at home too? Used by suicidal train staff when they see three thugs with their feet on the opposite seats.

→ *Op één been kun je niet lopen*. You can't walk on one leg. An excuse for having another one (drink).

→ *Kinderen die vragen worden overgeslagen*. Children who ask won't get anything. A good Calvinistic tradition that has fallen into disuse.

→ *Hoge bomen vangen veel wind*. High trees catch a lot of wind. People who distinguish themselves often attract criticism.

→ *Ben je in de kerk geboren?* Were you born in a church? Used when somebody doesn't shut the door when leaving a room.

→ *We stoken niet voor de kat zijn kut/viool!.* Another doozy regarding leaving doors open. We are not heating for the cat's cunt/violin.

→ *Die is niet goed in z'n bovenkamer.* He is not well in his upstairs room. Meaning he is nuts.

→ *Hij ziet ze vliegen*. He can see them flying. Meaning he is nuts.

Living in the Netherlands

Your First Steps

Central Station, Rotterdam

Visa, MVV and Residence Permit

Visa

Depending on your nationality, you will have to request a visa (called Visum Kort Verblijf (VKV), or Short Stay Visa) before entering the country if you want to come here for a period shorter than 90 days. Which countries these are, and how you go about arranging the visa, you will find on the website listed below.

MVV (Provisional Residence Permit)

If you want to come to the Netherlands for a period exceeding 90 days, you must arrange a provisional residence permit (MVV). To do this, you visit the Netherlands embassy in your country of origin or residence and initiate the so-called TEV procedure, whereby you apply for both an MVV and a residence permit at the same time. Here, they take your fingerprints and you hand in your passport photo. If you have a sponsor (a person or organization with an interest in your coming to the Netherlands, such as a family member, employer or university) in the Netherlands, your sponsor can start the TEV procedure, by filling in the application form, including the requested documents, and sending this to the IND.

You must await the decision on the TEV request abroad. Only under exceptional circumstances can you travel to the Netherlands before being issued the MVV: however, before doing this, you must report these circumstances to the IND.

If the IND decides that there is no objection to your entry in the Netherlands, it sends an MVV-approval to the Dutch embassy in your home country/country of legal residence. Before traveling to the Netherlands, you collect your MVV/provisional residence permit at the Dutch Embassy or Consulate in your home country/country of legal residence. Be sure to do this and travel to the Netherlands within three months after it is issued, for it must still be valid when you *collect* your definite residence permit in the Netherlands. Once you have arrived in the Netherlands you collect your residence document in person at the IND. Note: Below you will find the nationalities that do not need an MVV to enter the country. For all other nationalities it should be pointed out that you cannot apply for a residence permit if you entered the Netherlands without making use of the MVV.

An MVV must also be requested for your accompanying family members. Processing time is approximately 90 days.

MVV Not Required

The following persons do not need an MVV:
→ EU/EEA and Swiss Nationals: If you are a national of any of the European Union (EU) or European Economic Area (EEA) member states or Switzerland, you will not need an authorization temporary stay prior to traveling to the Netherlands. Formally, EU/EEA and Swiss nationals also do not need a residence permit; however, if you intend to stay here longer than four months, you will have to register with the municipality.
→ Some Non EU/EEA/Swiss Nationals: You are exempted from the need to arrange an authorization temporary stay if you are from the United States, United Kingdom, Canada, Japan, South Korea, Monaco, Vatican City, Australia or New Zealand.

Residence Permit (VVR–Procedure)

If you are exempted from the need to arrange an MVV, you can apply for a residence permit with the IND. Or your prospective employer can apply for the residence permit while you are still living abroad.

Required Documents

The documents that you have to submit when registering and/or applying for a residence permit are, among others:
→ a legalized certified copy of your birth certificate (also your spouse's or partner's)
→ a legalized marriage license, if applicable
→ if either you or your partner were previously married, a copy of the legalized divorce decree.

Whatever else you need depends on your circumstances and country of origin. Other documents, such as a passport, work permit and proof of insurance will be required at some later point, check with the IND what these are.

Registering with the Municipality

If you are planning on staying in the Netherlands longer than four months, you have to report with the municipality (*stadhuis* or *gemeentehuis*) to have yourself entered in the municipal register (*bevolkingsregister*). In order to be able to do this, you must first arrange 'suitable housing', which you demonstrate by means of a rental contract, purchase contract or a statement drawn up by the person in whose house you will officially be living.

Non-residents staying in the Netherlands for a period not exceeding four months also have to register, but as non-residents (RNI).

Town Hall Atrium, The Hague

If you are a national of an EU/EEA-country or a Swiss national and have legally resided in the Netherlands for a period of five years, you qualify for the residence document 'long-term residence of citizens of the Union'. You are, however, not *obligated* to request this.

Websites
→ Visa requirements: www.government.nl
→ MVV requirements: www.ind.nl/EN
→ Health insurance: www.government.nl/topics/
   health-insurance

DigiD

In order to file your online tax return, check out what your health insurance has paid for you, arrange benefits, order online municipal documents, etc., you need your digital identity, known as your DigiD. If you don't do any of this online, you can do without it – but what are the chances of that?

To arrange a DigiD, you have to register with the municipality in which you live, and make sure you have a *burgerservicenummer* (BSN). Then you visit www.digid.nl, where you fill in your *burgerservicenummer*, date of birth, postal code, and house number. Here you also choose a username and a password. Five days after you do this, you will receive your activation code by mail, which you must use within 20 days, together with your username and password, to activate your personal DigiD.

Citizen Service Number

Everyone who registers with a municipality in the Netherlands is issued a Citizen Service Number (*burgerservicenummer*, BSN) within a few days. Without this, your employer will not be able to withhold your social security contributions. Here, employers withhold these contributions and pay them to the tax authorities for you. You also need it to arrange your health care insurance and register with temp agencies.

Also expat family members have to obtain a Citizen Service Number.

If you are not a resident of the Netherlands or will be staying here fewer than four months, but need to deal with Dutch government institutions – for instance, because you are working here temporarily, or live abroad but receive a Dutch pension – you need to register with the Basisregistratie Personen (Basic Registration), which registers both residents and non-residents. You will be registered with the Registratie Niet-Ingezetenen (RNI, Registration of Non-Residents) and issued a *burgerservicenummer*. This you can use to arrange tax-related matters, but also benefits, such as the General Old Age Pension (AOW), if you live abroad.

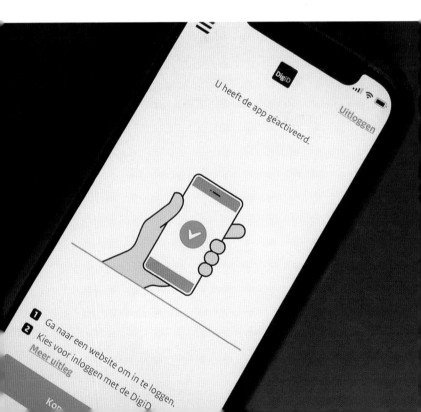

Refugees

If you have come to the Netherlands to seek asylum, you report with the reception center of the IND in Ter Apel (Groningen). There, you sign your asylum request, based on your personal situation, such such as fear of persecution or inhumane treatment, while the IND checks your identity and travel route. They also determine which procedure applies to you. After this has been done, the COA (Central Organization for the Reception of Asylum Seekers) places you in one of their locations, where you are assigned a lawyer and given a medical check. You are given six days to recover from your travel, during which time the IND plans your asylum procedure, you are given a more extended medical and psychological check, VluchtelingenWerk informs you about the procedure, and you meet your lawyer. The general asylum procedure lasts eight days; you tell your history and the IND judges your request. Sometimes the procedure lasts longer. Generally speaking, your hear the outcome within six months, though this can last up to 15 months.

If granted, you are issued a five-year residence permit. After these five years, the IND looks into whether to make this a permanent one.

This process is summarized in the infographic on the next page.

Working

If you have applied for asylum, you may not work during the first 6 months of your asylum procedure. After that you are allowed to work 24 of every 52 weeks, while the application is still being processed. You will need a work permit (TWV, issued by the UWV), which your employer applies for. You can keep 25 percent of what you earn, to a maximum of 185 euros. If you earn more than what you have to contribute to the COA, you can keep the rest. Volunteer work is permitted, based on a special permit, while no permit is needed to help out at the refugee center. You can also work in (self-)employment.

Procedure Seeking Asylum

STEP 1

You register with the Aliens police, submitting proof of identity. You are interviewed and given an initial medical test (which can include TBC).

STEP 2

You have an intake interview with the IND, accompanied by an interpreter.

STEP 3

You prepare for the interview with the IND. You are informed of the procedure and assigned a lawyer. A more extended medical / psychological evaluation takes place.

STEP 4

You are interviewed by the IND and explain your situation.

STEP 5

A decision is made within 8 days. Or you enter an extended procedure – this can last 6-15 months.

STEP 6

If the decision is positive, you are granted a 5-year residence permit. After 5 years, it can be extended. If the decision is negative, you have to leave the country within 28 days.

STEP 7

You can appeal the decision. This is decided upon within 4-6 weeks.

Studying

Those who have refugee status or are asylum seekers and are enrolling in higher education can approach Stichting UAF Steunpunt (www.uaf.nl) for more information on the possibilities of a grant. On their website, click on the little British flag in the top right-hand quarter to access more information.

Housing and Food

When you first enter the country, you are housed in emergency shelters, such as a sports center, a tented camp, an old school or a converted homeless shelter. All you have is a roof over your head and three meals a day, as well as toiletries and detergent. If you live in a refugee center, and have already entered the official procedure, you have a right to 60 euros a week for clothing and snacks – while you will also receive approximately 13 euros for additional expenses. One-time and other expenses are also compensated, such as for your children's (and your own) education, medical expenses, kitchen necessities, and asylum procedure-related expenses. Refugees who live independently receive between approximately 47 and 117 euros a week for meals, depending on whether they are alone or part of a family. If you live in a center, you receive 31 to 75 euros.

Bank Account

To open a bank account, you need a *burgerservicenummer* (BSN), a residence permit, or a refugee permit. The website given below explains the applicable procedures.

Education

As all children have a so-called 'education obligation', also refugee children will have to go to school. Every refugee center is linked to an elementary school, but the children are not obligated to attend this particular school. First they go to an international class, until their Dutch is good enough for them to attend the regular classes.

If you are not of school age, you are given lessons in the Dutch language, as well as additional courses, and receive help looking for a job.

Health Care

Every refugee has pretty much the same health insurance as Dutch citizens who take out the basic insurance. It is arranged by the COA and covers visits to the GP, antibiotics and maternity care (assistance after giving birth), as well as everything else the standard Dutch health care insurance covers. However, if you want to stop smoking, this is not covered...

Visiting a specialist becomes a little more complicated. Together with an insurance company, the COA has assigned a number of specialists to take care of refugees. However, to visit them, you must first request permission so that they can assess whether you really need to see one. (This is not any different for Dutch citizens; they need to see their GP first before being referred to a specialist).

Duties

As a refugee, you will have to report with the Aliens Police and the COA on a regular basis. You have to register with your municipality within six months. And all refugee centers have rules that you will have to respect.

Websites
→ COA: www.coa.nl/en/
→ Opening a bank account: www.mycoa.nl/en
→ Working: www.ind.nl/en
→ Studying: www.uaf.nl/home/english
→ General: www.vluchtelingenwerk.nl/english

Inburgering –
Integrating into
Dutch Society

O n the official Dutch government website – www.rijksover-
heid.nl – it is stated that the government is of the opinion
that it is important that anyone living in the Netherlands participate in Dutch society. For instance, by working here or studying
here. And that one condition for being able to do this is to learn
the language.

In fact, it states that if you are not from an EU/EEA country,
Switzerland or Turkey and are coming here for a longer period of
time, you are *obligated* to learn the Dutch language as part of the
obligated *inburgeringscursus*, which has been translated into
everything from the mild-sounding 'newcomers' course' to the
more off-putting sounding 'civic integration exam'. In any case,
the idea is for you to learn the language, get to know Dutch society
and find a way to become economically independent as quickly
as possible.

Of course, if you come here as a foreign student and follow one of the more than 2,000 English-language courses, then
you can probably get by just fine 'participating in Dutch society
as a student' without learning a whole lot of Dutch. The same
goes if you come here to work for an international company where
little, if any, knowledge of the Dutch language is required of you.
Furthermore, as everyone in the stores, bars and restaurants will
switch to English anyway once they detect an accent or a struggle
with the language, there will probably be no actual stimulus to
learn the language. Which is why it has been stated that anyone
who comes here temporarily – such as a student or an expat –
does not have to take the course.

The 'exam' has therefore been created for everyone who
wants to come here and build up a life. Before actually moving
here, depending on your nationality, you must take an exam (the
Basic Civic Integration Examination Abroad) at the Dutch consu-

late or embassy in your country of residence – or a neighboring country if your country does not have one – in order to be issued a provisional residence permit (MVV) with which you can legally enter the country. To do this, you register via the site www.naarnederland.nl (to the Netherlands), after which you can download an 'official self-study pack' with which to prepare for the three parts of the exam: Knowledge of Dutch Society, Speaking and Reading. Most questions are multiple choice and if you have passed one part of the exam, you do not have to redo it when you retake the parts you did not pass. Once you have passed this exam in its entirety, you are issued the MVV with which you can legally enter the country, register with the municipality you will be living in, and request a residence permit.

Once in the Netherlands, you take the second portion of the exam, which focuses on additional issues such as how to find a job, how to make an appointment at the hospital, and what types of schools there are (for if you have children). You have three years to pass the exam – if you don't, you receive a fine and you 'might be' refused a permanent residence permit. Refugees are not denied a permanent residence permit on these grounds.

Alternative to taking this exam is obtaining your diploma Dutch as a Second Language *(Nederlands als Tweede Taal)* or if you follow vocational training. For other exceptions and additional rules, you can check out any of the two websites listed here.

Dutch society is known as a 'caring society'; it helps drug addicts reintegrate into society, it protects prostitutes against disease and abuse, it is in the top-5 of countries that give the most to charity, and it pays out a lot of benefits to help those who (temporarily) cannot help themselves. In keeping with this mindset is the brochure for those whose partner wants to come live in the Netherlands too, in which you will find words to the wise such as: "Once in the Netherlands, they will have to get used to their new circumstances. You can imagine that homesickness, loneliness and a lack of social contacts could be among the problems your partner is faced with. There is always somewhere you can turn to with your or your partner's problems". And they go on to list a few. But that is not all; once your partner is here, and preparing for the exam, the brochure urges you to: "Practice with your partner, speak as much Dutch as possible with each other and ... explain the Netherlands and its customs to him or her". How many government institutions do you know that will take the trouble to place themselves in their immigrants' partner's shoes, so that they can advise the immigrant on how to help their partner integrate into society? And then sit down and write the text, have a meeting to agree that yes, this is how they want to put it, and then publish it? It is really quite endearing.

Other websites
→ www.inburgeren.nl
→ www.duo.nl/particulier/international-visitor/
→ Civic Integration Exam (*Inburgeringstest*):
  www.netherlandsworldwide.nl/civic-integration-
  exam-abroad

Obligation to Carry ID

Everyone over the age of 13 must carry some form of legal ID at all times; this being a passport (for EU nationals) or a valid aliens document (for non-EU nationals). Dutch nationals may show either a driver's license, a passport, or an identity card. Photocopies are not allowed, nor is inviting the police officer to your home to check your documents. Children over the age of 13 must have their own papers; inclusion in their parents' passport is not enough.

Who is authorized to ask you to show your papers? The police are, as well as parking inspectors, officers of the Health and Safety Inspectorate, inspectors from the Building Control Department, tax inspectors, customs inspectors, forest rangers (whom you will meet while walking your dog), school inspectors, etc. And, of course, but this is a totally different type of situation, you show your ID when opening a bank account, requesting a government benefit, starting a new job, etc. – AND when attending a soccer game...

The purpose of this obligation is to help combat crime and you may only be requested to show your documents if there is a valid reason – for instance, if you have committed a (traffic) offense or crime, are using public transportation without having paid for it, or if the police needs your assistance, for instance to help solve a crime, or to maintain the public order. The request must be in keeping with the position of the person asking you for your ID. In other words, a tax inspector cannot detain you for this purpose in connection with running a red light.

If you refuse to comply, you may be taken to the police station for identification and run the risk of owing a 2,250-euro fine (in extreme cases – in most cases, the fine will be more reasonable; more in the vicinity of 45 euros, for those younger than 16, and 90 euros for those older than 16).

Store and building security officers may ask you for your ID, but you do not have to show it. However, they are then allowed to deny you entry or to escort you out of the building.

Working in the Netherlands

A Job

In terms of number of jobs, the commercial services sector remains the strongest in the Netherlands, and has been for several years, closely followed by the health care and manufacturing industries. Also science & engineering are showing growth as they search for international and capable workers in areas such as water management, green and renewable energy, as well as logistics.

Dutch Employment Law

Unless you are working here under an expat contract governed by your home country laws, the Dutch rules on employment will apply to you. Even expatriates, whose contract explicitly states that a foreign law applies to the employment relationship, will find that they are subject to mandatory rules of Dutch employment, thanks to international private law. Let's take a look at a few topics.

Probation Period

Type of Contract	Maximum Duration of Probation
Contract for less than 6 months	no probation period
Contract between 6 months and for 2 years	1 month
2-year or permanent contract	2 months

Chain Contracts

Chain contracts sounds rather vague, but what the term refers to is a chain of employment contracts for a limited period of time. In order to protect employees against employers who try to avoid offering them a permanent employment contract by means of a series of temporary ones, it has been decided after three consecutive fixed-period contracts – or if the fixed-term contracts exceed three years in total – the employment contract is deemed to be a contract for an indefinite period of time, even if it is explicitly stated that it is a fixed-term contract. If you first work for an employer via an employment agency and then directly for this same employer, the first contract – through the employment agency – counts as the first contract of the chain of three.

Only if a period of more than six months has passed between contracts is this fictional 'chain' broken and does the counting start from the beginning. These rules do not apply to certain types of work, nor to employees who are younger than 18 years of age.

Min/Max/Zero Hours

If you work on call, there are two types of contract you can enter into. One is min/max contract: this offers you a guaranteed number of hours of work (and pay) as well as the possibility that your employer will call you in to work more hours, to a predetermined maximum. Every time you are called in, you receive a minimum of three hours' pay, if you have a contract for a maximum of 15 hours and the hours are not fixed. It offers you certain rights that all employees have, such as continued pay (70 percent) during illness, protection against dismissal, and the accrual of holiday allowance, as well as the obligation on your side to show up if you are called in – provided you are given at least four days' notice that you will be expected. If your employer cancels less than four days in advance, they must pay you for this gig. After the first 12 months have passed, your employer is obligated to offer you a contract for the average number of hours you worked over these 12 months.

There is also the 'nul-uren contract' (zero hours contract), which does not offer a minimum number of hours, but does require your employer to pay you at least three hours every time he calls you in. It can be for a limited or an unlimited period of time. If you have worked for this employer longer than six months, then you have a right to wages if, for instance, there is no work or your employer does not call you in through there *is* work.

Dismissal

If something has happened that has damaged your work relationship, your employer has to terminate the employment contract via the sub-district sector of the District Court (or Cantonal Court). If the reason for dismissal is long-term illness on your side, the employment contract can be terminated via the UWV (Employee Insurance Agency). Other ways to terminate an employment agreement are: by mutual consent, during the probationary period, or through summary dismissal for 'urgent cause'.

Dismissed employees have a right to a so-called transition compensation. See below.

Notice Period

When terminating the employment contract, your employer must apply the following notice periods (unless the employment contract is dissolved by the courts, or unless the end date is linked to a specific project or temporary replacement of another employee):

Length of employment period	Notice period
0 – 5 years	1 calendar month
5 – 10 years	2 calendar months
10 – 15 years	3 calendar months
> 15 years	4 calendar months

If you have a temporary employment contract of longer than six months, your employer must notify you one month in advance. For temp contracts with a duration of less than six months, termination can be with immediate effect.

For you, the employee, the notice period is always one month. You can agree differently, in which case the agreed-upon notice period for the employee is doubled for the employer. Collective labor agreements (CAOs) can provide for different (and even equal) notice periods.

Severance Payment/Transition Payment

Severance payment can be granted either as a lump sum (known as a 'golden handshake'), or as a periodically paid supplement to the unemployment benefit or lower wages in the next job. This so-called transition payment (*transitievergoeding*) is calculated as follows: 1/3 of your monthly salary for every year of employment if you were employed, plus an additional formula applied to the number of days that exceeded the complete years (for instance, if you worked six years and four months).

Employment Agency

Employment agencies are expected to treat you equally to employees who are in the employment of the company to which you are sent to work when it comes to wages, working on holidays, night shifts, overtime, vacation days, compensation, etc.

The collective labor agreement (CAO) of the ABU (Federation of Private Employment) applies to foreign temps, also those who have been recruited to work in the Netherlands via an agency. You can find the details of this CAO on the ABU website, in English, Polish, German, Arabic and Turkish. The site is listed below. It applies to all employment agencies, thus also to (foreign) employment agencies that place employees on the Dutch labor market from abroad. Furthermore, nationals of the European Economic Area (EEA) can move to the Netherlands for work and enjoy the same conditions as Dutch nationals in areas such as access to housing, wages and social security – among others.

Language

Unless you have been sent here by a company and will remain working in an English-language (or any other foreign language) environment, you probably won't be able to get by without learning Dutch. In fact, the government has determined that if you work in a 'risky' work environment (manning large machines, or removing asbestos, for instance), you have to be able to speak Dutch, in order to be able to function safely and avoid accidents. The level of your job and responsibilities will determine the level of Dutch required.

The ability to speak English fluently, however, will often come in handy in this internationally-oriented economy. But don't forget, the Dutch speak the language quite well, so it won't be enough to land you the job!

For more on language courses, see our pages on *Learning Dutch*.

Don't forget to check out the rules on work permits, in our item *Work Permits*, and the need for a BSN (*burgerservicenummer*).

Websites

Collective Labor Agreement Foreign Temp Agencies

→ www.abu.nl

Finding a job

→ www.linkedin.com

→ www.monsterboard.nl (in Dutch)

→ www.intermediair.nl (in Dutch)

→ www.stepstone.nl (in Dutch and English)

→ www.iamexpat.nl/career/jobs-netherlands

→ www.expatica.com (in English)

→ www.togetherabroad.nl (in English)

→ www.oneworld.nl (in Dutch)

→ www.jobbird.com (in Dutch)

→ www.nationalevacaturebank.nl (in Dutch)

→ www.vacatures.fd.nl (in Dutch)

→ www.yer.nl

Work Permit

EU/EEA/Switzerland

If you want to work in the Netherlands, you will need a work permit, unless you are a citizen of an EU/EEA country or Switzerland. There are also special conditions for US and Japanese nationals.

Single Permit

If you are a national of any other country and want to work here longer than three months, you will have to request a GVVA (Gecombineerde Vergunning voor Verblijf en Arbeid, Combined Permit for Living and Working), which you request from the Immigration and Naturalization Services (IND). This also applies if you come here to gain work experience as a trainee or apprentice.

Work Permit

You do not need a GVVA, but do have to request a work permit from the UWV (Dutch Employee Insurance Agency) if you:

Container terminal, Port of Rotterdam

→ are staying here shorter than three months
→ have come here to do seasonal labor
→ are a student
→ are a refugee
→ have been sent here by an international group of companies.

Further Conditions

If you are not from an EEA-country, you can only work here if the employer cannot find someone suitable to do the job within the EEA, the job has been on the market for at least five weeks (or, as the case may be; three months), and the employer can show he has done his utmost to find someone on the EEA market.

Further Exceptions

You don't have to arrange a work permit if:

→ you come here as Knowledge Migrant (see further on)
→ your residence permit states that you are free to work here
→ you have come here to set up a start-up (you are given a year to do this)
→ you are self-employed and are doing work that is listed on your residence permit
→ you in principle require a work permit, but are working here in the employment of a service provider to whom the free movement of employment applies (for instance, another European country).

On the website of the IND, you will find more categories.

Students

As a non-Dutch (PhD) graduate or scientific researcher, you can stay/come here to look for a job after graduation. The following conditions apply:

Graduated here	Graduated abroad
Time to look for a job: 1 year	Time to look for a job: 1 year
Upon graduation, you have three years to stay here and look for a job	Upon graduation, you have three years to come here and look for a job
Also applies if you have a Bachelor's Degree	Does not apply if you have a Bachelor's Degree
Must show a certified copy of the diploma	Must have the diploma valuated by Nuffic
You must be able to support yourself during this search – else you could forfeit your permit	You must be able to support yourself during this search – else you could forfeit your permit

Once you have found a job, your employer must initiate the GVVA-procedure, requesting both a work permit and a residence permit. If you meet the requirements for being a Knowledge Migrant, you request a residence permit for Knowledge Migrants. If you start your own company, and meet the conditions, you change your residence permit to one for self-employed persons and you do not need a work permit. If you are an EU/EEA or Swiss national, you are free to work here. If you have to do an internship as part of your Dutch studies, you do not need a work permit, however you do need one if you come in from abroad.

Knowledge Migrants

In order to improve the position of the Netherlands as a knowledge economy and to make it more attractive as a work location for Knowledge Migrants from outside the EU/EEA, it has created a policy aimed at simplifying their entry into the country. To enter the country as a Knowledge Migrant, you need either an MVV and a residence permit or, if you do not need an MVV, merely a residence permit. You do not need a work permit. Only a recognized sponsor, your employer, can submit a request for this with the IND.

Also guest lecturers, scientific researchers and medical trainees are regarded as highly skilled migrants.

European Blue Card

The European Blue Card has been created for non-EU employees who come to carry out highly qualified work in the EU. The conditions are stricter than those for Knowledge Migrants. You can find these on the website listed below.

The Blue Card not only allows you to work in the Netherlands without the need for a work permit, but after 18 months you and your family can live and work here, and elsewhere in the EU, as well.

Spiritual Counsellors or Ministers of Religion

Special rules apply to these persons. They can be found on the IND website.

Family Members

If you have a partner or relative who has permission to live and work in the Netherlands, you may be able to obtain a residence permit for the purpose of family reunification, which would give you the same rights as your family member. If they have permission to work, you *may* be exempt from the need for a separate work permit.

Please note! If a family member who is not an EU/EEA or Swiss citizen, intends to stay with you in the Netherlands, you have to register with the IND.

A Few Other Rules

- If you **change employers**, the new employer must also have a work permit in your name
- The single permit is issued for up to three years
- A work permit is **valid** for the duration of your employment contract, up to a maximum of five years, but can be extended
- **Students** can work while studying, but there are restrictions for non-EU/EEA/Swiss nationals: you can only work up to 16 hours per week, or full-time for seasonal work in June, July and August. In both cases, your employers will need a work permit in your name. There is no limit on the number of hours you wish to work in self-employment

- If you don't need a work/single permit (combination residence permit and work permit), you can work as soon as you have your residence permit, which you can collect as soon as you arrive in the Netherlands
- To carry out research at a recognized **research** institute, your institute applies for a residence permit for scientific research on your behalf. You do not need a work permit to carry out the research work but if you take on any other type of work in addition, then the employer will need to obtain a work permit in your name
- To work here as an **au pair**, you must go though an au pair agency approved by the Dutch immigration authorities. The agency will arrange a year-long residence permit for you, including permission to work (for more information, see website listed below)
- If you want to work here in **self-employment**, you will need an MVV or a residence permit (for more information, see website listed below)

Websites
→ Conditions Highly Skilled Migrants:
www.ind.nl/en/residence-permits/work/
highly-skilled-migrant
→ Working in the Netherlands after graduation:
www.ind.nl/en/residence-permits/work/residence-
permit-for-orientation-year
→ Traineeship/apprentice/work placement:
www.ind.nl/en/residence-permits/work/trainee-or-
apprentice-in-the-netherlands
→ Conditions European Blue Card:
www.ind.nl/en/residence-permits/work/apply-for-a-
residence-permit-european-blue-card
→ Family reunification:
www.ind.nl/en/residence-permits/family-and-partner

Starting Your Own Company

If you are orienting yourself on becoming an entrepreneur, or at least self-employed, these pages offer you some helpful tips.

Chambers of Commerce

The Chambers of Commerce (Kamers van Koophandel) register (practically) all companies based in Holland, whether they are of Dutch or foreign origin. Private persons who work on a free-lance basis and persons who carry out one of the professions specified on the professions list of the Chamber of Commerce, are also obligated to register.

The Chamber of Commerce has an information desk that can provide you with information on how to start a business, which diplomas you need for your specific line of business, how to write a business plan to be able to finance your ideas and what (zoning) plans your municipality has within the area in which you want to establish your firm.

MKB-Nederland

MKB-Nederland (Instituut voor Midden- en Kleinbedrijf) represents the interests of small and medium-sized companies. Various activities are initiated by this institute, aimed at offering its members relevant knowledge and expertise as well as at improving the general position of small and medium-sized companies.

Banks and the national tax office have information desks for people who plan to start their own business and can provide you with the information you need. The banks might be able to offer you financial assistance as well. All major cities have a business desk at the town hall. An excellent step–by–step guide in English can be found on: www.answersforbusiness.nl/guide/starting–business

Proof of Identity

When registering with the Chamber of Commerce, you need to bring valid proof of identity (such as a passport, residence permit or driver's license) and a rental contract for your office. An appointment can be made online, at that time you can check what else they might need to register you. together with an original private bank statement or an original extract from the population register (not older than one month).

Setting Up Establishment

There are no specific restrictions for foreign companies who wish to start a business in the Netherlands, nor are there restrictions on the ownership of real estate or on the remission of capital and profits abroad.

There are various legal entities that you can set up:

→ branch office
→ *eenmanszaak*: a one-man business
→ *maatschap*: partnership – business involving more than one person, usually used by accountants, doctors, etc.
→ *vennootschap onder firma* (Vof): general or commercial partnership – business involving more than one person, under a common name, each severally liable

- → *commanditaire vennootschap* (CV): limited partnership with managing and 'silent' partners
- → *besloten vennootschap* (BV): private company with limited liability
- → *naamloze vennootschap* (NV): (public) corporation.

Taxes self-employed persons

If you run your own business you can be held liable for the following:

- → wage tax
- → income tax
- → national insurance schemes
- → employee insurance schemes
- → VAT (value added tax).

If you run a one-man business, you only owe income tax and VAT.

Health Care Insurance

You must arrange your own medical insurance, for which you owe a fixed contribution and an income-dependent contribution. If your income lies below a certain level, you can apply for government assistance in paying for this insurance, called the *zorgtoeslag*.

VAT

If you deliver services and goods in the Netherlands, you are obligated to charge your customers VAT (*Belasting Toegevoegde Waarde* or BTW), which you subsequently pay to the tax authorities. The general VAT rates are 21 percent and 9 percent. You owe this, no matter whether you (aim to) make a profit or not, the moment an invoice is sent out. To the delivery of goods and services outside the Netherlands, other rules apply.

The amount of VAT that you have paid to others who deliver their goods and services to you, can be deducted from the amount of VAT you owe. If your 'VAT income' does not exceed a certain amount, you enjoy a full or limited exemption from paying the amount due to the tax authorities.

The amount of VAT due should be reported on the *Aangifte omzetbelasting*, or Turnover Tax Return, on a regular basis (monthly, quarterly or yearly). This is done online, by means of the so-called electronic, or *electronische*, Tax Return. The tax authorities issue you a username and a password to do this.

DBA

According to Dutch law, you are an employee if you have a boss who can tell you what to do, AND you have to do it yourself AND you are paid wages for it. In that case, your employer has to withhold certain taxes for you and pay them to the tax authorities. If one of these elements is missing, you are not working in employment, but rather in self-employment, and these taxes do not have to be withheld. To make this official, you and your client can enter into an agreement, for which the tax authorities have provided a variety of models. You are not obligated to make use of such a contract – it just offers you and your clients more clarity.

In order to avoid taxes, some might agree with their client that they are working in self-employment, when in fact they are not. The Tax Authorities will take action if they feel the following situations arise:

→ there is a (fictitious) employment relationship
→ there is obvious false self-employment
→ there is intentional false self-employment.

If it is found that you were not working in self-employment, your client will have to pay the taxes due over the period you worked for them, either of you may owe a fine and you may no longer work for this client, unless the client draws up an employment agreement.

Tax Deductions

There are a variety of tax deductions, which you can find on the site of the tax authorities. These include a deduction for self-employed persons, a starting entrepreneurs' deduction, a starting disabled entrepreneur's deduction, among others.

Also, tax credits are available for investments made in cultural investment funds, green funds and socio-ethical funds.

Diplomas/Permits

Depending on the type of business you want to start, there are a number of diplomas you might need. For most types of businesses, however, no diploma is required. Keep in mind that some businesses are subject to a zoning plan, or require a building permit, environmental permit or establishment permit. Before you start your business, contact your municipality or the Chamber of Commerce to find out which permits and/or diplomas you may need.

If you have obtained a diploma in another country, this diploma can be evaluated by IDW (www.idw.nl), to see whether it qualifies.

Free-Lancing

There are two ways you can go about free-lancing; either as a self-employed person or through an employment agency. In the first case, you can read about some of the rules that apply to you in these paragraphs; in the latter case, you are, in principle, treated as an employee of the employment agency for tax purposes.

Websites
→ Starting a business: www.answersforbusiness.nl/guide/starting-business
→ Registering with the Chamber of Commerce (Kamer van Koophandel): www.kvk.nl/english/

Money
matters

Social Security

I f you legally reside and/or work in the Netherlands, you are (in principle) subject to the Dutch social security system, as is your partner/spouse and/or other members of your family. This is only different if you are exempt under EC Regulation 883/2004 or a bilateral social security treaty.

There are two kinds of compulsory social insurance schemes in the Netherlands; one that is applicable to the population in general (national insurance schemes) and one that is applicable to employees only (employee insurance schemes).

The National Insurance Schemes

There are five national insurance schemes (*volksverzekeringen*):

→ General Old Age Pensions Act (AOW) Those who are covered by the AOW are entitled to an old age pension upon reaching the age of 65+. Over the past years, this was raised incrementally, until it reached 67 in 2021. It is accrued between the ages of 15 and 65.

→ General Surviving Relatives Act (ANW) This is a widow's, widower's or 'dependent children'-benefit, and is income dependent. The deceased spouse, partner or parent must have been insured under the ANW at the date of his or her death. There is a long list of who is *not* insured, but if you work in the Netherlands, pay taxes here and do not have a Posting of Workers Certificate (secondment agreement), you are covered by this insurance.

→ Long-Term Care Act (WLZ) This act makes a provision for those who need intensive care or supervision 24/7. For instance, elderly persons with dementia, or persons with severe mental, physical or hearing/seeing disabilities. It includes treatment and nursing in recognized institutions and nursing homes, personal care and nursing, the supply of artificial appliances, medical care, and transportation to the place of supervision or treatment. In order to receive this care, the person must be approved for this type if care. They are then issued a so-called *WLZ-indicatie*.

→ **The Health Insurance Act (ZVW)** Pursuant to this act, everyone who legally resides in the Netherlands and is subject to the Dutch social security system is obligated to have health insurance. You can read more about it in our item on *Health Insurance*.

→ **Child Benefit Act (AKW)** This benefit (*Kinderbijslag*) is paid out to parents who have children under the age of 18. The amount of the allowance depends on the age of the child and special rules apply to children age 16 and 17.

Contributions (Payable to Tax Department)

Contributions for the national insurance schemes are levied on income up to approximately 35,500 euros a year, together with the income tax.

If the total of any of the benefits and any other family income is less than the minimum income, you can apply to the Social Security Institution for a supplement under the Supplemental Benefits Act (*Toeslagenwet*). These benefits are paid out specifically to help finance rent, health care insurance premiums, daycare for the children of working parents, and general expenses related to the having of children.

Employee Insurance Schemes

There are four employee insurance schemes (*werknemers-verzekeringen*).

→ **WULBZ/ZW (In case of illness)** Pursuant to the WULBZ, your employer is obligated to continue paying 70 percent (up to a maximum of 70 percent of the so-called daily wage) of your salary during the first 104 weeks of sickness, provided you have a contract governed by the Dutch civil code. Some employers pay a higher percentage or even 100 percent of your last-earned salary.

The ZW is a 'safety net' for certain categories of employees, such as employees who do not – or no longer – have an employer (for example temporary workers), and employees who have taken out a voluntary ZW-insurance. Sick pay is usually 70 percent of the daily wage and is paid out a maximum of 104 weeks.

→ **Work and Income According to Labor Capacity Act (WIA)** The WIA applies if you have been disabled for work for more than 104 weeks. The aim of this act is to stimulate 'ability' for work. It makes a distinction between long-term disability for work (no recovery within five years), temporary complete disability (80-100 percent) and partial disability for work.

→ **Disability Insurance Act (WAO)** The WAO only applies to employees who were already receiving the WAO-benefit on January 1, 2006.

→ **Unemployment Insurance Act (WW)** The WW insures you against the financial consequences of unemployment. It lasts a minimum of three months and depends on your employment past. You must have lost at least 5 hours of work a week, be immediately available for work, worked at least 26 of the past 36 weeks and not be responsible for the fact that you lost your job. Be sure to have yourself informed on your accrued rights and over how long you will receive this benefit.

Contributions (Payable to Tax Department)

The contributions for the employee insurance schemes are levied by the tax department, together with the wage tax.

Exceptions

EU/EEA/Switzerland

You are not subject to the Dutch social security legislation if you have been posted from another EU or EEA (European Economic Area) member state or Switzerland, or if you work here shorter than six months – unless your income earned in the Netherlands is subject to wage tax here, and you in fact carry out your work here.

There is a whole set of rules surrounding continued coverage of the social insurance system of another EU/EEA/Swiss country; but they are too detailed to go into here. For more information, visit www.belastingdienst.nl, under *Payroll Taxes*.

If the Netherlands has entered into a social security treaty with the country from which you have been posted, this treaty determines which applicable social security legislation applies to you. If you are here temporarily, you will probably continue to be covered by the social security system of the country from which you have been posted.

If you have been posted from a country with which the Netherlands has not entered into a social security treaty, it is – in general – not possible to obtain an exemption from the Dutch social security system.

Websites

→ Social Security in international situations:
   www.belastingdienst.nl/wps/wcm/connect/en/
   individuals/individuals – search for Social Security
→ Benefits: www.belastingdienst.nl/wps/wcm/connect/
   en/individuals/individuals – search for Benefits
→ Sociale Verzekeringsbank (Social Insurance Bank):
   www.svb.nl

Taxes

Yes, taxes are high in the Netherlands. But these taxes are not used to support King Louis XVI's life in Versailles, or to expand upon King Charles I's paint collection. Instead, a lot of them go right back into our own pockets.

As soon as your child is born, you receive a quarterly amount to help you pay for their needs. Has your child turned 18, which means that this quarterly amount has stopped? No need to worry: he/she can now request a monthly payment – a gift – that amounts to more than the initial benefit. The vast majority of university studies cost 2,000 euros a year in tuition. You can't afford your health insurance, which is already a lot cheaper than in most other countries? The government will help you out. You can't afford to pay rent? Ask the government for their support.

Plus the multitude of other benefits and government support measures, as well as tax deductions that you can benefit from.

So, that is where a lot of your tax money goes.

Resident Taxpayer

How is it determined whether you owe taxes, and how much you owe? The first question that has to be answered is: are you a resident taxpayer or not? The answer to this is found by evaluating the following points: where do you have your home, where does your family/partner live, where do you work, how long have you lived in the country, what other ties do you have with it?

Tax Boxes

If, based on the above, it is determined that you are a resident taxpayer, then you owe taxes over your entire worldwide income, wherever you earn it (tax treaties may determine differently). There are three 'boxes' over which taxes are due: income from real estate, benefits, shareholding, etc.; income from substantial shareholding; and income from savings and investments.

Tax Rates

→ Box 1 In this box, there are four tax brackets, divided into approximately 0-20,000 euros (taxed at 37 percent); 20,000-33,600 euros (taxed at 41 percent); 33,600-57,600 euros (also taxed at 41 percent); and more than 57,600 euros (taxed at 52 percent) (tax percentages are approximate, as they change annually, at least behind the comma).

→ Box 2 Taxed at 25 percent.

→ Box 3 Taxed at 30 percent over 4 percent of the assets, creating an effective tax rate of 1.2 percent.

Partners

Taxpayers who (these conditions are not cumulative):

→ are married or registered partners

→ have a civil partnership agreement drawn by a civil law notary, including a 'mutual care stipulation'

→ have a child together
→ jointly own their main residence
→ are considered partners in a pension scheme

are considered partners for tax purposes. This means they can allocate common sources of income and deductible items – such as mortgage interest for the principal place of residence, medical expenses or study costs – to each other's tax return in such a way that they can reap the maximum benefit from them.

Non-Resident Taxpayer

As a non-resident taxpayer, you only pay income tax on income from certain sources in the Netherlands, such as: Dutch business income, employment income, income from real estate in the Netherlands and income in the form of periodic benefits, and a substantial shareholding in a Dutch company. In most cases, employment income that you earn while you are physically not in the Netherlands is not taxed here.

Partial Non-Resident Taxpayer

This is only an option if you are benefitting from the so-called 30%-ruling (we'll get back to that). In that case, you are a resident of the Netherlands for income (and deductibles) in box 1, but you are treated as a non-resident in boxes 2 and 3.

'Real' Non-Resident Taxpayer

If you are a non-resident, but you earn your income in the Netherlands and would like to benefit from the available deductibles, then you can choose this option. Be sure you consult a tax advisor, before making this decision.

30%-Ruling

You can make use of the 30%-ruling tax facility if you have been posted from or recruited outside the Netherlands to work in the Netherlands. For this, you do not need to be a resident of the Netherlands and you do not have to (physically) carry out work here, either. The ruling allows your employer to pay you a tax-free allowance of up to 30 percent of your wage for so-called 'extraterritorial expenses' – expenses you would not have had,

had you not been sent/placed abroad – as a result of which the effective rate of wage tax is reduced.

There are further conditions that must be met for this – your tax consultant can tell you more.

Double Taxation

As mentioned earlier, you may find yourself owing double taxes. In order to help you avoid this, several countries have entered into tax treaties with each other. In keeping with most of them, you do not owe taxes over income from employment in the Netherlands if:

→ you are in the Netherlands for, in total 183 days (approximately six months) in any 12-month period or in a fiscal year, and

→ your wages are paid by or on behalf of an employer who is not a resident of the Netherlands, and

→ your wages are not borne by a permanent establishment or permanent representative of the employer in the Netherlands.

For countries with which the Netherlands has not entered into a tax treaty, there is a unilateral arrangement. This will often mean that income earned abroad is exempt from taxation in the Netherlands, although it will be taken into account for the purpose of calculating the (progressive) tax rate applicable to your further income, which is then taxed in keeping with the 'normal' rules.

Websites
→ www.belastingdienst.nl
→ www.belastingdienst.nl/wps/wcm/connect/en/ individuals/individuals

Insurance Matters

You cannot legally reside in the Netherlands without medical insurance. So let's get you started on figuring it out.

Health Care Insurance

To pay for health care insurance, everyone pays a fixed contribution to the insurance company and an income-dependent contribution to the tax authorities. This income-dependent contribution is compensated by your employer, who pays it directly to the tax authorities. If you receive a benefit or old age pension, it depends on your social security institution or pension plan whether your income-dependent contribution is compensated.

TIP Health care insurance is free for children under the age of 18.

If you are unemployed or self-employed, you receive no compensation. You receive an annual preliminary assessment for the amount you owe, which is based on what the tax authorities estimate you will be earning that year. If you end up paying too much, you will be reimbursed after the final tax assessment over the year in question.

Deductible

There is a fixed deductible (see further on); by increasing the amount of the deductible, you can decrease the income-independent part of your contribution. It does not apply to children until the age of 18, visits to the GP, visits to the midwife, maternity care, care covered by voluntary additional insurance or dental care for children/persons until the age of 21.

Selecting an Insurance Company

All insurance companies are obligated to accept all applications, regardless of age, gender or health. The cost of a basic insurance is pretty much the same across the board; doing a little comparative shopping becomes worth your while if you are interested in additional coverage – or eliminating certain coverage.

However, insurance companies are not obligated to take you on for additional coverage and can refuse you additional health care insurance.

TIP The government offers financial assistance (called *zorgtoeslag*) to persons (also self-employed) whose income lies below a certain level, to help pay the health care insurance premium.

You can change insurance companies every year. Issues to look at when doing comparative shopping are: the amount of the deductible, coverage while abroad, level of dental care offered, alternative therapies, etc.

Types of Policies

When you are arranging your insurance, you will run into the terms '*natura polis*' or '*restitutie polis*'.

→ If you take out a *natura* policy, your insurance company will pay your medical bills directly if you go to a medical service provider with whom they have entered into a contract with (you are free to select your own *huisarts*, or GP). If you visit a specialist/therapist with whom no such contract exists, they will only cover a portion of the expenses.

→ The *restitutie* policy is slightly more expensive, but does give you freedom of choice as to whom you wish to turn to for medical assistance. Often you pay the bill yourself and then submit it with your insurance company for restitution.

→ The cheapest insurance policy is one that is close to the *natura* policy; if you visit someone with whom the insurance company does not have a contract, they do not have to cover the costs at all.

If you are traveling within Europe, ask your insurance company to issue you your European Health Insurance Card (EHIC), which will allow you to receive free medical care (or at a reduced cost) in any of the other EU/EEA countries and Switzerland, if treatment becomes necessary during your visit or if you are suffering from an existing chronic condition.

Some insurance companies offer a combination of the two types of insurances, and with many insurance companies you will find they are not excessively strict about the existence of an actual contract between them and the care provider, provided the care provider is recognized by a professional organization.

Long-Term Medical Care

The WLZ (Wet Langdurige Ziektekosten, or Long-Term Medical Care Act) is a national insurance scheme that insures persons against risks that cannot be covered by individual insurance. Everyone who legally resides and works in the Netherlands has a right to coverage by this insurance. It is meant to cover steep medical expenses. You owe a contribution for this insurance over income from (self-)employment.

Dental Care

Dental care is not included in any basic package (with the exception of dental care for children up to the age of 18 and 'specialist' dental care, including dentures). Braces are usually covered up to a certain percentage.

Medication

In your policy you are likely to find something along the lines of "we only cover GVS medication". This refers to the fact that types of medication have been 'clustered', after which a maximum price has been determined for this cluster. If you are prescribed medication, then the cluster-specific maximum price is covered by the insurance. If your medication is more expensive than that, you will have to pay the difference.

Check with your insurance company whether you can take out an additional policy to cover these extra costs as well as the costs of homeopathic/alternative medication.

Pregnancy and Childbirth

Visit to your midwife are covered by your insurance, as are at least two ultrasounds, if they are medically required.

Home child birth is covered by your insurance. The costs of a hospital delivery are fully covered if it has been determined

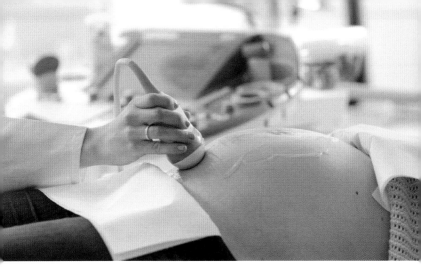

that, for health and safety reasons, the baby should be delivered in the hospital. If you voluntarily choose to have your baby in the hospital (called a *poliklinische bevalling*), you might have to contribute towards the costs of your hospital delivery. For more, see *So You're Pregnant*.

Students

Students who come to the Netherlands merely to study cannot take out Dutch health insurance. Your host institution might already have arranged insurance for you – though you should verify this, of course. Special packages for students are available. If you have an EU Health Insurance Card, which you can get if you are insured under the (public) health care scheme in your (EU) home country and your stay abroad is temporary, you will continue to be covered by this insurance policy. It is up to your health insurance provider to determine what constitutes a temporary stay if you go abroad to study. Once you start working on the side, you may have to check if there are any further conditions.

Website
→ Health care insurance shopping:
   www.zorgwijzer.nl/zorgvergelijker/english

A Place to Stay

Renting a Home

Y ou might find yourself unpleasantly surprised by rental prices in the Netherlands, but it is worth realizing that, compared to prices elsewhere in Europe, they are quite reasonable. What might be more of a surprise, are the modest sizes of the apartments and the steep stairs leading up to them – or to the other stories in your house.

Types of Rental Properties

Basically, there are three different types of property you can rent:
→ Unfurnished (*Ongemeubileerd*). Or empty; no carpeting, no curtains, often a minimum of or no appliances and no utilities.
→ Semi-furnished (*Gestoffeerd*). Some furnishings and carpeting, and possibly a few appliances. Do ask for a complete list of what is included. Utility inclusion or exclusion depends on the landlord.
→ Furnished (*Gemeubileerd*). Everything has been taken care of and the apartment is ready to be moved into. It may contain any combination of furniture, appliances, curtains, light fixtures, carpets, cutlery and dishes, television, stereo equipment, kitchen appliances such as microwave, dishwasher, refrigerator, and sometimes even bed linens and blankets or duvets. Once again, ask for a complete inventory list before agreeing to anything. If anything is missing, negotiate it before you sign the lease. Utilities are (usually) included.

Many rental contracts have been especially designed to meet the needs of expatriates, and include an English translation.

The Rental Contract

A rental contract usually includes the following items:
→ rent: payable one month in advance
→ a deposit: usually one month, sometimes 2 or 3

→ an annual adjustment of the rent, based on increases in the cost of living, as determined by the Central Bureau of Statistics (CBS)

→ user's costs, such as utilities, municipal levies and garden maintenance

→ diplomatic clause, see the next paragraph

→ brokerage fee

→ a clause on minor repairs

→ a clause stating that the lessee is responsible for the yearly cleaning of the central heating system, water boilers, chimneys, gutters and draining pipes

→ the obligation to return the property in the same condition, normal wear and tear excepted, at the end of the rental period – or else forfeit (a part of) the deposit.

Generally, regardless of the cause of the damage, the lessee pays 200 euros, excl. VAT, per case. All costs of larger repairs, external or internal, which are not due to any fault of the lessee, are paid by the owner.

TIP Do a careful walk-through of the house or apartment you are planning on renting, to verify existing damages and the need for repairs and improvements. Put in writing who will be responsible for arranging and paying for these repairs, etc., before you sign on the dotted line.

Diplomatic Clause

It *can* happen that you have rented a property, but are sent to another location or country before the rental contract comes to its end – or that the owner, who rented it out to you because they were sent abroad, is brought back home by their employer. In these situations, one of you will have to able to terminate the rental contract before the agreed term is over. In order to be able to do this, make sure you include a diplomatic clause in your rental contract, which gives either of you the option of terminating the contract after a notification term mutually agreed upon in advance, should this be necessary.

TIP There are two types of rental contracts; for an indefinite period of time or for a maximum of two years.

Checking In

Once you have signed the contract and been handed over the keys, you are checked in by the owner or their representative, assisted by their own agent. A checklist is filled out regarding the condition of the house, the furniture, fixtures and fittings belonging to the house, the condition of the exterior/garden, and the inventory. The house should be thoroughly cleaned, including the inside of kitchen and bathroom cabinets. The inspection report as well as the inventory list must be signed by the lessee and the lessor.

Terminating the Rental Contract

There are two types of rental contracts; for an indefinite period of time or for two years. If you have a contract for an indefinite period of time, you – as a renter – cannot terminate it during the first year. After that, you can terminate it by giving between one to three months' notice and you enjoy full protection against having to leave the home. If the lessor wishes to terminate the contract, the notice period is between three to six months, depending on the duration of the contract, but you do not have to leave, unless the court decides otherwise.

If you have a two-year contract, your lessor will have to 'remind' you of the end of the two-year rental period between one and three months in advance. You can terminate the rent any time you want, provided you give at least one month's notice, but the lessor cannot. If you do not notify your lessor that you are leaving, you will at the very least forfeit your deposit (usually two months' rent) if you move out anyway. If, after the initial two-year rental period, the rental contract is not terminated, it undergoes a *stilzwijgende verlenging* or silent continuance and becomes contract for an indefinite period of time, meaning you will enjoy full protection against having to leave the home.

Either agreement should be confirmed in writing and notice should be given by registered letter.

Checking Out

Usually on the last day, an official check-out will take place, checking the inventory and condition of the lease property with the checklist made when you moved in. If the state of the property is found to be satisfactory and all bills in connection with the property have been paid, the deposit will be paid back within three months after the check-out date. If necessary, the costs of restoring the rental property back to the required state will be deducted from the deposit in accordance with the bills provided by the lessor.

Taxes

There is no tax facility for renting a house. If your employer chooses to compensate you for the housing costs, this will be considered taxable income if you are a (partial non-) resident taxpayer. Whether you will have to pay the tax yourself depends on whether your contract is net or gross.

If you benefit from the 30%-ruling, a part of the rent may be qualified as an 'extraterritorial expense' (you can read more about this in the chapter on *Taxes*). That part of the rent can be compensated free of tax.

If you are a non-resident of the Netherlands, any compensation of double housing expenses is considered compensation for extraterritorial expenses: tax-free, but resulting in a reduction of the 30 percent allowance.

Buying a Home

Real Estate Agent

Though you can go a long way on your own with the help of the Internet, we advise you to contact an agent for the actual house-search and negotiation phase. Besides the fact that they have access to a computerized multiple-listing system which keeps them completely up-to-date on properties available in their district, they are familiar with the price ranges, local contracts, 'invisible' obligations, laws and customs, as well as the local bidding systems, zoning plans (*bestemmingsplan*), soil contamination and city council regulations.

Real estate agents charge a brokerage fee (*courtage*) for their services of approximately 1 to 2 percent of the purchase price of the house, though it can be negotiable. Some offer an expat service package.

Advantages and Disadvantages of Buying

Aside from the fact that the value of your house might go up by the time you sell it, there are a number of other advantages as well:

→ You get a tax relief on the mortgage interest if the house is your principal place of residence, provided you take out an annuity or straight line mortgage.

→ A number of the costs related to the financing of the house are also tax-deductible, such as: some of the civil law notary's fees, the closing commission, and the fee for the appraisal of the house.

Disadvantages are:

→ You pay approximately 6 percent of the purchase price as one-time buyers' expenses. These expenses consist of a transfer tax, estate agent fees, civil law notary's fees, a fixed fee for the bank or broker, etc.

→ You must add the so-called deemed rental value (*eigenwoningforfait* – we'll get back to this) to your taxable income and pay taxes over this.

Points to Keep in Mind

→ Once you have a real estate agent, ask him to advise you on matters such as environmental laws, the survey of the house, hidden defects, and issues surrounding leasehold vs. freehold.

→ The purchase price excludes furniture, carpets, curtains, light fixtures and sometimes kitchen appliances. You can negotiate which goods could be included in the purchase.

→ You pay a deposit of approximately 10 percent of the purchase price of the house which is due approximately five weeks after the deal has been made. It is to be paid to a civil law notary and can be part of the financing agreement reached for the purchase of the house.

→ If you will be taking out a mortgage, make sure the purchase agreement is subject to financing.

→ Other resolutive conditions can be included, such as being able to obtain a permit to occupy the real estate, or even more importantly, the option of having a constructional survey carried out.

If you need the assistance of an interpreter when communicating with the civil law notary, you are legally required to request the assistance of a sworn interpreter. Depending on your language, this will cost you anywhere between 150 and 500 euros.

What Type of Mortgage?

You should seek proper advice on the type of mortgage that is suitable in your situation, particularly in view of the limited period of time during which you may need the mortgage. Do not forget to inform the bank if you are benefiting from the 30%-ruling. If you come here as an actual expat, the two major tax issues with which you will be faced are the 30%-ruling and the choice between resident and partial non-resident tax status. Be sure to get expert advice!

Deemed Rental Value and WOZ-Value

Those who own a house and use it as their principal place of residence have to report a certain amount – related to the home ownership – on their income tax return. This amount is a percentage of the value of the house, and is called the *eigenwoningforfait* (or deemed rental value). The *eigenwoningforfait* based on the official value of the house, also known as the WOZ-value, which is determined every year by the municipality.

When looking for a contractor, visit the BouwGarant website. Under *Woonplaats*, you fill in where you live and then click on *Zoek aannemer* (find contractor). Be sure to invite a few *aannemers*, as prices can vary considerably.

Preliminary Tax Refund

The balance of the deemed rental value and the interest can be deducted from your income. You can receive a tax refund on the mortgage interest deduction every month by requesting a preliminary negative tax bill from the tax authorities. The tax authorities will then deposit the refund directly into your bank account.

Local Taxes

If you own a home, you will also find yourself paying local, municipal taxes. These will amount to approximately 2,000 euros a year.

Exemption from Customs Duties

If you transfer goods from a non EU-country to an EU-Member State (such as the Netherlands), you are subject to customs duties, VAT and other special taxes (for example excises and a special tax on cars). A special exemption can provide relief in these circumstances if you meet certain conditions.

Usually your removal company can take care of the related administrative obligations.

Find out whether your house is a 'monument'. If it is, you will be subject to strict rules regarding maintenance, painting and reconstruction.

Websites
Looking for a home
→ www.funda.nl
→ www.jaap.nl
→ www.pararius.nl
→ www.zah.nl

Contractors
→ www.bouwgarant.nl

Real estate agents portals
→ www.makelaars.net: real estate brokers portal
→ www.makelaars-nederland.nl: real estate brokers portal
→ www.mva.nl: Makelaars Vereniging Amsterdam
→ www.nvm.nl: Nederlandse Vereniging van Makelaars

The Process of Buying a House

→ You select a real estate agent, and discuss what you are looking for, what you need and what is realistic.

→ If you have any special wishes regarding the property, make sure your real estate agent and the real estate agent of the seller are aware of this. If they are not, and it turns out your home does not meet these wishes, you cannot hold them accountable for it.

→ You contact a mortgage provider, to find out exactly how much mortgage you can take out, whereby you take into account additional expenses involved in the purchase of the home and, if applicable, the fact that you fall under the 30%-ruling.

→ You visit property.

→ When you have found a home you like, be sure discuss all issues such as city council regulations, but also issues such as soil contamination.

→ If you want this home, you can inform your real estate agent of this verbally.

- → Your real estate agent will contact the selling party and relay this message.
- → Have a building inspection carried out. If you fail to do this and there is a problem, more likely than not, you will have lost your right to hold the seller accountable.
- → Make the purchase of the house contingent upon its passing the building inspection.
- → The initial verbal agreement you reach with the seller is put in writing in the preliminary purchase contract. A penalty clause is usually included in case the seller or the buyer does not meet his obligations.
- → After being signed by all the parties, the preliminary purchase contract is sent to the civil law notary who deals with the transfer of the title of the house.
- → A three-day 'cooling-off' period starts the day after the buyer receives a copy of the signed contract. During these three days the buyer can cancel the deal without any repercussions and without having to state the reason.
- → The civil law notary inspects the public registers of the Land Registry regarding mortgages and/or attachments with which the property may be encumbered.
- → The transfer of ownership takes place at the civil law notary's office by means of a deed of transfer that is drawn up by the civil law notary and signed by the seller, the buyer and the civil law notary. You will receive a draft of this deed and of the mortgage deed beforehand. Also your agent will receive these and check them.
- → The agent will check together with you to see whether the house has been vacated, and is in the agreed condition.
- → The civil law notary takes care of the financial settlement of the transaction and ensures that the deed of transfer is entered in the public registers (Land Registry).
- → The transfer then becomes official and you receive the keys of your new house.

Setting Up House – Monthly Expenses

When you have bought your home, there are a number of things you will be wanting to arrange, such as utilities, telephone, TV, insurances and, while you're at it, let's start with a bank account.

Bank Account

To open a bank account, you first have to decide which bank you want to work with. In alphabetical order, you will probably consider the following banks: ABNAmro, ING, Rabobank, SNS, Triodos – though there are more! Next, you visit the bank's website to make an appointment at a bank office, or you can set up a bank account online. In both cases, someone from the bank will call you, either to inform you on what you need to bring, or else to help you set up a bank account after verifying your data. Once this has been arranged, you will receive a debit card, with an activation code and a pin code, by mail. You can use the debit card to make payments in stores, with the use of your pin code.

Credit cards can be arranged through your local bank or directly through a credit card company.

Insurance

You can arrange your house-related (as well as other) insurances via the same bank: home insurance and household contents insurance, but also legal liability and valuables. The cost is calculated based on where you live, what you insure, what it would cost to rebuild your house and your deductible. You pay a fixed amount per 1,000 euros of insured value. A home contents insurance will cost you between 10 and 19 euros a month and once again mostly depends on the insured value and where you live.

Liability insurance covers any damage you, or your children, cause to other persons or their property. Insuring 1,000,000 euros, with no deductible, costs three to five euros a month, for a single person, and six to eight euros per month for a family with children. It is a modest monthly premium to pay for accidents that, as the Dutch say, 'lie in a small corner' (meaning: small mishaps can have big consequences).

Utilities

A goodly amount of your income will go to utilities – gas and electricity. Shop around to determine which company offers you the best rates, because they tend to vary. In most cases, the providers determine how much they think you will have to pay them on a monthly basis, depending on whether you live in an apartment, a detached house, a semi-detached house, a house on a corner of a row of houses, or a house in the middle of a row of houses – and how many people live in your household. They will send you this estimate, and if you want, you can lower or raise it online. If you pay too much, they return it to you (and make a new, lower, estimate for the next year) and if you pay too little, you are presented with an additional bill (and a new estimate). Other factors taken into account are where you live, and for how long you take out the contract. The cost varies from approximately 70 euros, for one person in an apartment, to 210 euros for four persons in a detached house – though plenty of people end up paying a whole lot more than 210 euros! It depends, of course, on how resistant you are to the persistent cold of the Dutch winters.

There are two types of contracts; fixed and variable. The fixed ones don't change their rates for the duration of the contract (one, two, or three years, for instance), but the variable ones adjust their rates every six months. In case of uncertain global circumstances, such as the Ukraine war in 2022, only very few companies offer fixed rate contracts.

So-called 'green' – or sustainable' energy is also available. You can find companies that supply this on the site of the Consumers' Association (www.consumentenbond.nl).

Water

For the water you use, you pay an amount to your local water supplier. For a four-person household, this will amount to approximately 22 euros a month.

Local Taxes

Another goodly amount of your income will go to local taxes: waste collection tax, municipal property tax, water board assessments, sewerage charges, etc. Some of these charges are fixed, others are calculated based on the value of your home.

The average annual taxes come down to 1,265 euros to the municipality, 750 to the province and 340 to the *waterschap* (water control corporation). Though this can be quite a bit higher, depending on where you live. As a renter, you owe less; approximately 360, 255 and 280 euros a year.

Telephone and Television

A combined subscription for telephone and television will cost you between 32 and 82 euros month, depending on the MBs involved and any additional features, such as television-on-demand, HBO, etc.

A Car

The monthly expenses involved with having a car in the Netherlands include not only, obviously, gasoline and insurance, but also Road Tax (*motorrijtuigenbelasting*). The amount depends on the weight of your car, the province you live in, the type of fuel, etc. and, for the average car, will range from 35 to 280 euros.

If you own a car or a motorcycle, you are legally required to take out *Wettelijke aansprakelijkheidsverzekering*, or *WA-verzekering*, to cover any damage you cause to another person or person's property. You can also insure damage to your own car, in which case you can choose between *beperkt casco* and *volledig casco* (or all-risk). *Volledig casco* includes damage caused by an 'outside force', such as fire, theft, storm, slipping on ice, collision, etc. – even if it is your fault that this 'outside force' impacted your car. With *beperkt casco*, you are not covered for damage that you have caused yourself, yet you *are* covered for fire, theft, storm, a collision with an animal, and glass breakage. The price of car insurance varies, depending on the level of coverage you opt for – as well as where you live, the type of car, how many claim-free years you accumulate over time, etc. The average car insurance costs approximately 30-90 euros a month.

A Cell Phone

You can take out a monthly subscription with a cell phone or buy a separate phone and take out a so-called sim-only subscription. Or you can take out a pre-paid subscription. The cheapest sim-only subscriptions start around 11 euros, the cheapest subscriptions start at 10 euros, but you add a certain amount depending how much you decide to pay up-front for the phone, if you buy one through the provider. The cheapest pre-paid subscription will get you 10 euros worth of 10-cent-a-minute calls, or 10-cent-a-text message. Once you add MBs, this will bring you up to 16 euros a month, in combination with above rates.

Websites
Utilities Comparison
→ Gaslicht: www.gaslicht.com
→ Independer: www.independer.nl
→ Keuze.nl: www.keuze.nl
→ PartnerPete: www.partnerpete.com
→ Pricewise: www.pricewise.nl
→ Overstappen: www.overstappen.nl
→ Utility Provider: www.utility-provider.nl

Energy Label

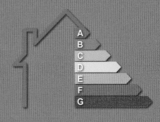

For quite a while now, cars and household equipment have been issued an 'energy label', ranging from A – G, to indicate how energy-efficient they are. A is the most efficient, G the least. All houses/apartments must also carry an energy label (also called *energieprestatiecertificaat*), to be issued by a certified advisor, which is valid for a period of ten years and is handed over with the sale or renting out of the house/apartment. The energy label also takes into account the type of house and provides information on how energy can be saved, making it easier to compare the energy efficiency of houses. It runs from green (A++++) to red (G). If you cannot show this label, you will not be able to sell your house, while renters will owe less rent, and you will owe a 435-euro fine.

This is all part of the government's aim to become one of the cleanest and most energy-efficient countries within Europe. Measures that influence the classification of your house are, for instance: roof insulation, double glazing, and a ventilation that allows the recuperation of heat. Though you are not obligated to take measures to improve the rating of your house, doing so may contribute to increasing its value, while you might be able to get a more favorable mortgage. The government's website www.verbeterjehuis.nl offers suggestions for improvement and subsidies.

The cost of obtaining the energy label depends on the size and type of house. In the case of apartment buildings, a rebate may be possible, while, in the case of 'similar houses' an 'example house' of the series may be used as a basis. Nonetheless, a separate certificate must be issued for each house. A certified advisor can be found by visiting www.energielabelvoorwoningen.nl, and following the steps on this site. You will need your DigiD (or digital identity) to do this. As the site is in Dutch, you might wish to enlist the assistance of your realtor to arrange the energy label.

Education

Should You Choose an International Education or 'Go Dutch'?

Before enrolling your child at a school, you'll have to decide whether to send them to an international school or 'go Dutch'. Both have their own advantages, which you can read about here.

Length of Stay in the Netherlands

If you are planning to stay in the Netherlands for a short period, an international school may provide your child with a greater sense of continuity.

If you are planning on staying for a longer period, and would like your child to mix with the local culture and learn the Dutch language, you may prefer to choose a Dutch school.

Your Child's Age

Another factor to consider is your child's age. In the first two years of Dutch school (ages 4-6), the focus is on learning through play, Dutch language acquisition, social and motor skills, and gradual preparation for reading and writing. 4 and 5-year-olds who don't speak Dutch can usually start a regular Dutch school straight away. They normally pick up the language quickly and are (almost) fluent before formal reading and writing starts at age 6.

Foreign children aged 6 and older are usually required to follow a Dutch immersion program before starting regular school. This takes about one year, after which they can continue their education with children of the same age at a Dutch school.

Difference in Cost

The third factor is the huge difference in cost. Apart from a few private, fee-paying schools, all Dutch schools (primary, secondary and tertiary institutions) are government-funded. Parents pay a small contribution with which the schools pay for a few extra things.

Some international schools are partly subsidized by the Dutch government, while others are completely private. For a subsidized school, the annual fees are about 5,500 euros per child, while for private international schools they can go up to 26,000 euros a year.

Curriculums

A unique feature of the Dutch school system is the choice in type of education. Among the state-funded schools there are some religious schools (Catholic, Protestant, Christian, Islamic, Jewish) or those that follow specific philosophic or pedagogic principles (e.g. Montessori, Waldorf). All schools are obligated to adhere to the government's 'core objectives', which specify what all pupils in all schools need to accomplish each year. The individual schools may fill in the specific details.

You'll also find some schools with a **bilingual curriculum** (usually Dutch and English). These schools vary in the amount of time they teach in English, and usually require a child aged 6 or older to have a decent level of Dutch, before they can join classes with Dutch-speaking peers.

International schools normally either follow the curriculum of the country they are related to, or use the theme-based **International Primary Curriculum** (IPC). A few international primary schools make use of the inquiry-based **International Baccalaureate** (IBPYP) program. As this program is expensive, many international schools only follow the IPC program in primary years, and then the Middle Years Program (MYP) and Diploma Program (DP) in secondary years.

Holidays

The Dutch school attendance law is very strict. From age 5, your child is only allowed to miss school for very specific reasons, e.g. a family emergency or important celebration. International schools are often a bit more flexible in allowing their pupils to take time off during term time, although absences due to extended holidays or early departures at holiday times are usually strongly discouraged.

The summer holiday in Dutch schools lasts six weeks. During the school year, there is at least one week of holiday after each period of about six weeks, so that both pupils and teachers can recharge their batteries. International schools either follow the holiday periods of the country they are related to, or set their own schedule. Pupils at international schools usually enjoy longer summer breaks than their Dutch peers, but often don't have the frequent breaks throughout the year, and their school days are normally longer.

Foreign Families in Dutch Schools

Contrary to international schools, most Dutch primary schools don't give homework till the higher classes. This means that, as a non-Dutch speaking parent, you won't need to worry much about not being able to help your child with homework. As the schools' approach and experience with non-Dutch families differs greatly, it is always good to find out about this before you choose a school.

Secondary Education

At Dutch schools, the pupils take the 'Central End Test for Primary Education' in the last year of primary school (ages 11 or 12). This is a standardized aptitude test with questions testing their Dutch language and comprehension skills, mathematics, study skills, and (optionally) world orientation.

Before this test takes place, the teacher assesses what level of secondary school education (see below) would fit each pupil best. They base their recommendation on various factors including the pupil's test scores from lower classes, intelligence, attitude towards learning, eagerness to learn and interests. The assessment of the teacher is the deciding factor.

Insufficient Dutch language skills can negatively impact a child's secondary school recommendation. If a child is motivated to improve their Dutch, and wants to attend a higher school level than their recommendation, there is the option of attending a one-year *Kopklas*, focused on the Dutch language. At the end of *Kopklas*, the child will hopefully get a recommendation for a higher school level than they had the previous year.

The different types of secondary schools, from lowest to highest academic ability, are as follows:

→ **VMBO** Preparatory secondary vocational education: 4 years, followed by MBO (Intermediate Vocational Education)
→ **HAVO** Senior general secondary education: 5 years, followed by HBO (*Hogeschool*/University of Applied Sciences)
→ **VWO** Pre-university education: 6 years, followed by (research-oriented) university (= WO)

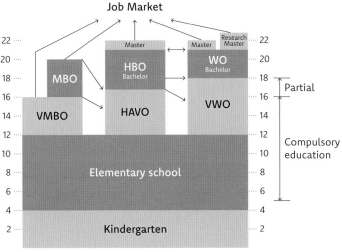

Bron: http://en.wikipedia.org/wiki/Education_in_the_Netherlands

Many secondary schools have a mixed-level 'bridge class' in the 1st year. Secondary education generally continues till the ages of 16-18, depending on the level, as seen above. After obtaining a diploma from one level (for example HAVO), you may proceed to the next level (VWO). Likewise, after completing HBO you may continue to university. For some university courses in the Netherlands, you can only enroll if you have followed a particular program during the last years of secondary school, for example Culture & Society, Economics & Society, Nature & Health, and Nature & Technology.

Most universities worldwide accept students with a VWO diploma. Sometimes they have additional requirements, for example proficiency in the local language and/or having passed the VWO exam with high grades. Higher education is offered at a high standard in the Netherlands; all 13 state-funded Dutch universities score well in The Times Higher Education World University Rankings.

International Secondary Education

International schools at secondary level often offer the IBMYP (ages 11-16) and IBDP (ages 16-19) curriculums. The IBDP is a globally-recognized high standard diploma, valued at the same level as a Dutch VWO diploma, and gives access to a research-oriented university. It is possible that a Dutch university requires proof of Dutch language proficiency, and/or a pass in a certain subject examined at secondary level. However, there are plenty of courses at Dutch universities that are completely in English.

The IB Organization has also developed a new curriculum for the final two high school years, as an alternative to the IBDP; the IBCP (International Baccalaureate Career-Related Program). It offers secondary general and vocational education, and the diploma has been validated by the Dutch authorities to be comparable to at least a Dutch HAVO-diploma with vocational subjects. The IBCP incorporates the IB-principles in a program created for students who want to focus on career-related learning, thus providing them with both an academic and practical foundation. Currently, the British School in the Netherlands (BSN), the International School of The Hague (ISH) and AICS in Amsterdam offer the IBCP track.

Websites
→ www.New2nl.com
→ www.eseng.nl - special education needs
→ www.sio.nl - list of all international schools
→ www.dutchinternationschools.nl – for a complete current listing of international schools

Going to University

The higher education system in the Netherlands is based on a three-cycle degree system, consisting of a bachelor's, master's and PhD degree. It is offered at two types of institutions: research universities (WO) and universities of applied sciences (HBO). Research universities primarily offer research-oriented programs, and universities of applied sciences offer programs of higher professional education, which prepare students for specific professions. They tend to be more practice-oriented than the programs offered by research universities.

53.4 percent of the population between 30 and 35 have a higher education degree; 49.1 percent of men and 57.8 percent of women.

'Research' Universities

Academic education (*universiteit*) universities are organized around a bachelor's or undergraduate phase that lasts three years and a master's or graduate phase that lasts one to two years. An overview of English-language university studies can be found on www.studyfinder.nl.

Groningen University

As many Dutch universities have partner institutions in other EU countries, students can follow part of their course abroad.

Hogescholen or 'Universities of Applied Sciences'

HBO (*Hoger Beroepsonderwijs*, or Higher professional education) focuses on applied arts and sciences in one of the seven HBO sectors: agriculture, engineering and technology, economics and business administration, health care, fine and performing arts, education/teacher training, and social welfare.

There are over 2,100 international short, bachelor's, master's and PhD-courses on offer – 99 percent of which are taught entirely in English. The site www.studyfinder.nl offers international students a complete overview.

The universities of applied sciences offer four-year bachelor's degree programs as well as master's programs lasting one to two years. All degree programs focus on preparing students for particular professions and are more practically-oriented, often requiring students to complete an internship or work placement (*stage*).

International Education

Next to the research universities and universities of applied sciences, Holland has a third and smaller branch of higher education, officially known as 'International Education' (IE), which offers advanced training courses, taught in English, originally designed for people from developing countries whose jobs require highly specialized knowledge. Most of the IE institutions are part of a research university and focus on courses relevant to developing countries.

A number of university centers offer Dutch as a second language-courses. The courses are specially designed for foreign students who have otherwise qualified for admission to Dutch higher education, but must first master the language.

Requirements for Admission

For access to WO bachelor's programs, students are required to have an IB-diploma, a VWO-diploma or to have completed the first year (60 ECTS, see further on) of an HBO program. The minimum access requirement for HBO is an IB-diploma (and, in some cases, the IGCSE-diploma with two additional subjects at GCE-level), the IBCP diploma (though be sure to double-check this), the Dutch HAVO/VWO-diploma or a level-4 MBO-diploma.

A quota, or *numerus fixus*, applies for access to certain programs, primarily in the health sector, and places are allocated using a weighted lottery. Potential students older than 21 years of age who do not possess one of the qualifications mentioned above can qualify for access to *To determine whether your diploma qualifies, if you have a non–Dutch secondary school– diploma or an IB– diploma, you must have your diploma evaluated by your prospective educational institute.* higher education on the basis of an entrance examination and assessment. The only access requirement for the Open University is that applicants be at least 18 years of age.

Doctorate

All research universities in the Netherlands are entitled to award a PhD. The process by which a doctorate is obtained is referred to as the *promotie* and the minimum amount of time required to complete a doctorate is four years.

Candidates with foreign qualifications may apply for these positions and ask for permission to write their dissertation in another language. You can also contact a university faculty independently, and write your own research proposal and sometimes the research for a dissertation can be conducted in your own country.

Choosing a University

The Dutch system of quality control guarantees that the education offered at all the institutions meets the same high standards. Instead, students look at which specializations are offered and which emphasis or academic tradition is featured.

To double-check the quality of the institution you are considering, visit the NVAO website listed below.

Language

To enroll in a program or course that is conducted in English, you must have the appropriate level of command of the English language. To determine this, you must take an English language test, such as TOEFL, IELTS, or CAE/CPE.

Making the Transition

In order to prepare for studying the Netherlands, there are three additional options. Contact your university to see what options there are for you:

→ You are allowed come here for a year first to study Dutch.
→ You can come here for a year to follow a preparatory program for the particular studies of your choice.
→ A transitional year that has been created for specifically for non-European, non-Western students to help them prepare for their studies here, this is called a *schakeljaar*.

On our following pages: Practical Matters for Incoming Students.

Websites
→ The Dutch higher education system:
www.studyinholland.nl/education-system
→ English-language studies: www.studyinholland.nl
→ Quality control: www.nvao.com
→ Schakeljaar: www.uaf.nl/ondersteuning/ik-wil-studeren/schakeljaar

For a complete overview of the master's degrees available in the Netherlands www.theofficialmasterguide.nl

Practical Matters for Incoming Students

Tuition

From a tuition point of view, there are two types of institutions of higher education: those that are government-funded and those that are government-approved. Studying at a government-funded institution will cost approximately 2,200 euros a year (first-year students pay half), for EU/EEA/Swiss/Surinam-students. Students of all other nationalities generally pay higher fees, on average 8,000 euros – though it can go up to upwards of 15,000 euros, depending on the length and level of the program.

Residence Permit

To be granted a residence permit for study purposes, you must follow a study at a recognized school or university (of applied sciences). All Dutch educational institutes must apply for the residence permits on behalf of their foreign students; you are not allowed to do this yourself. They request this at the same time they request an MVV (provisional residence permit) for you, with which you will be allowed to enter the country. Upon arrival you pick up your residence permit at the IND – as the MVV merely allows you to enter the country and is only valid for 90 days. You will also have to register with the municipality (registration GBA).

If you are an EU/EEA-national, you do not need a residence permit, but if you stay here longer than four months, you need to register with the municipality.

Health Care Insurance

If you are under the age of 30 and here solely for the purpose of studying, you do not need to take out Dutch health care insurance. If you are insured under the public health care scheme in your (EU) home country and your stay abroad is temporary, you will probably continue to be covered by this insurance policy. It is up to your health insurance provider to determine what con-

stitutes a temporary stay. You can request an EU Health Insurance Card (EHIC) to prove that you are insured.

You can find more about insurances in the insurance section on www.studyinholland.nl/plan-your-stay/insurance. It covers situations such as internships, having a job and working in self-employment while a student.

Internship/Work Permit

If you have a residence permit for studying in the Netherlands, and you have to do an internship here, you do not need a work permit. You do need to arrange the standard internship agreement.

If you are not studying in the Netherlands, and want to come here to do an internship or to acquire work experience, then if you are a non-EU/EEA/Swiss national, you will need a work permit.

A Job on the Side

As a student, you are allowed to work a maximum of 16 hours a week, or full-time during the months of June, July and August. Your employer will need to apply for a work permit. EU/EEA/Swiss students can work as many hours as they like, without the need for a work permit.

Finding a Job After Graduating

If you are a graduate of a foreign university, you can come to the Netherlands for a period of one year to find work as a highly skilled migrant. You can read more about this on our pages on *Work Permit*.

Costs of Daily Living

Your daily expenses will include tuition, rent and daily expenses, as well as basic health insurance, obtaining a permit, transportation (unless you qualify for a public transportation pass, see further on), books, notebooks and perhaps membership fees for student (sports) organizations. You can expect all this to amount to approximately 800 euros – 1,300 euros a month, though this of course depends on the amount of tuition you owe. Housing will cost you between 300 euros and 600 euros a month.

Housing

It is hard to find proper housing. If you are participating in an exchange program or are enrolled in an international course, it is quite possible that housing has been arranged for you by the institution. If your institution has not actually arranged housing for you, they often have special departments for foreign students that help them find a suitable place to live.

There are a few national and international student organizations that can help you find internships, work placements and temporary jobs, as well as fun and interesting activities. The most important ones are AEGEE and AIESEC.

Once you have found a place to live, what can you expect? In Holland, students usually have their own room. You might have to share the shower, toilet, kitchen and living room with other students, and it is common for men and women to live together in a shared house.

Finances

Most banks will probably be willing to support you financially and to answer any finance-related questions you may have. Ask about their loans. At least the following banks have special programs for students: ABN Amro, ING, Rabobank and SNS.

If you would like to take on a paid job alongside your studies, you will need a *burgerservicenummer* (BSN, Citizen Service Number). You are issued one automatically when you register with your municipality. If you are a non-EU/EEA/Swiss citizen, you will also need your student residence permit and a work permit.

Grants

To find out more about scholarships, also for non-EU students, and whether you qualify, visit www.grantfinder.nl. Here you can enter your field of study and your country of origin and see for which grants or scholarships you might qualify. Also

check ScholarshipPortal.eu or contact your university in the Netherlands to find out whether it has a grant for international students, as some have their own grant programs.

Those who have refugee status or are asylum seekers and are starting a higher education can approach Stichting UAF Steunpunt (www.uaf.nl) for more information on the possibilities of a grant.

Studiefinanciering

If you are younger than 30, registered for a full-time or a dual education, and have the same rights as a Dutch national, you can apply for student finance (*studiefinanciering*). *Studiefinanciering* is made up of four elements: a loan, a public transportation card (*OV Studenten chipkaart*), an additional loan and a tuition fee loan (*collegegeldkrediet*). All of these amounts must be paid back, with the exception of the additional loan and the public transportation card, which you will not have to pay back *provided* you obtain your diploma within ten years.

The amounts change annually, but basic loan lies around slightly more than 513 euros a month; the additional

TIP Be sure to arrange a DigiD (your digital identity), in order to arrange your *studiefinanciering/* tuition fee loan online!

loan depends on your parents' financial situation and is a maximum of approximately 419 euros a month, while the tuition fee loan is approximately 184 euros a month.

More information can be found on the website listed below. There you will also find when you have the 'same rights' as a Dutch national as well as more about limited funding assistance if you do not meet the requirements.

Going Abroad

You can 'take' your *studiefinanciering* abroad with you, subject to conditions you can find on the DUO website.

Websites
→ Daily expenses: www.studyinholland.nl/practical-matters/daily-expenses
→ Student finance (*studiefinanciering*): https://duo.nl/particulier/international-student/
→ Refugees/asylum seekers: www.uaf.nl
→ Study grants: www.studyinholland.nl/finances
→ Scholarships: www.scholarshipportal.eu

Getting
Around

Amsterdam Central Station

Public Transportation

Trains

The Netherlands has a dense railway network that offers frequent service, as well as the quickest way to travel between city centers. The carriages are modern and clean and, although many Dutch people complain about delays, the trains usually run on time. (Everything is relative!)

The Dutch trains have first and second class compartments. First class costs about 50 percent more and the seats are slightly larger and less likely to be full.

If you are not traveling using a public transportation card (see further on) and want to buy a one-time train ticket, you can buy this ticket on the website listed below or in the 9292 app.

High Speed Trains

You can travel by high-speed train (the Thalys or the TGV) from Amsterdam, Schiphol or Rotterdam to Belgium and – final destination – Paris. If you are going to Germany or Switzerland, you can take the high-speed ICE train, and if you are going to London, there is the Eurostar – though you have to travel to Brussels, Belgium, first to catch it. These high-speed trains are really only a worthwhile option if you intend to travel all the way to these far-away destinations as, within the Netherlands, the trains still travel at regular speeds through the densely populated areas. Only once they reach France, do they pick up speed. In other words, don't count on cutting time by taking the high-speed train from Amsterdam to Rotterdam.

You can only travel on a high-speed train if you have bought a special (more expensive) ticket for this train and have made a reservation. If you accidentally board the Thalys in Amsterdam to go visit you friend in Rotterdam and you are caught, you will be fined!

The Public Transportation Card – OV-Chipkaart

There two types of public transportation card, or *OV-chipkaart*: the personal *OV-chipkaart* and the so-called anonymous *OV-chipkaart*. The personal *OV-chipkaart* is a plastic credit-card shaped public transportation card with your photograph that contains information on the amount of credit it still has on it, on whether you have a right to certain reductions, and on whether you are traveling on the basis of a public transportation 'subscription', or pass. You can find travel discount products on the website listed below.

USEFUL APPS
NS travel, 9292, CityMapper and De Betrouwbare OV Fiets App (for renting a public transportation bicycle).

Tourists can buy an anonymous *OV-chipkaart* or a disposable *OV-chipkaart* at the station (at an NS ticket automat), a supermarket, a newsagent, on the tram/bus, at the airport, or a public transportation company. The anonymous card can be used for more than one day and/or longer distances, the disposable card for a single use or short period.

You can also buy train tickets online, on the site listed below.

TIP Do not forget to load credit onto the *OV–chipkaart* before using it! You can do this at the counter of a public transportation company or at the NS ticket automat at the train station, on one of their yellow devices. It will require a certain minimum amount before it will approve your trip.

Using the OV-Chipkaart

When entering the platform at the train station, you hold your card against the card reader (either a white pole with the dark pink oval that says *Kaart hier*, or a yellow pole with the grey circle and an illustration of the card that says *OV-chipkaart*). When you get off the train and leave the station, you do the same.

In the buses and trams, you hold the card against the card read just inside the door as you go in and as you go out. If you forget to check out, you can visit the website listed below to see if you can fix this.

Students are issued a public transportation pass, this is a 'product' that can be linked to/downloaded onto their personal *OV-chipkaart*. You can choose whether you want to travel for free between Monday morning 4 A.M. and Saturday morning 4 A.M. (and at a reduced price during the weekends, on holidays and during summer break) or for free between noon Fridays and Monday 4 A.M., as well as holidays and summer break, and at a reduced price on weekdays. It is considered a loan that you don't have to pay back if you graduate within 10 years. More information can be found on the website listed below.

TIP You cannot use a credit card to buy an *OV-chipkaart*.

Even though you use the same pass to travel by train, bus and tram (metro), you need to check out of each one before you get on another one! Largely, this does not apply if you switch trains, but it does apply if you go from traveling by train to say, traveling by bus. When does it apply when traveling by train? When you switch companies: to a regional train company, such as Arriva or Connexxion.

Passes

There are a wide variety of passes and special tickets that can save you money when using public transportation. Which type you choose depends on the kind of traveling you will be doing – frequent or infrequent, long distances or short, alone or in a group, during rush hour or not, and your age. One source of information is www.ns.nl/en/travel-information/.

Taxis

You cannot hail taxis on the street in the Netherlands like you can in many parts of the world. You must either request one by phone, or go to a taxi-stand where taxis wait. All major railway stations have a taxi-stand. Hotels and restaurants are always happy to call a taxi for you if you ask.

Schiphol, Amsterdam Airport

The regular Dutch taxis use meters and charge roughly the same rates. When you start, the meter will already show a balance of several euros. This ensures the driver a minimum fare. Only for very long distances is it sometimes possible to negotiate a fare in advance. It is customary to give taxi drivers a tip, which usually means increasing the amount up to a round figure.

There are also regional taxis that you can share with other passengers, thus reducing the cost. Just a few tips: you request the taxi an hour in advance, you can expect him to arrive anywhere between 15 minutes earlier and 15 minutes later, you can only travel within the region (20-25 km), you can expect (obviously) other passengers, and you pay approximately 4 euros per 5 km. If you receive a WMO-benefit, you travel at a reduced rate. Another option is Zone Taxis, see the website listed below.

Uber is available in the bigger cities in the Netherlands.

Schiphol Taxis

Below you will find a site on taxi services to and from Schiphol Airport, as well as a hotel shuttle for Amsterdam.

Websites

→ Information and purchase *OV-chipkaart*:
www.ov-chipkaart.nl (click on *English*)
→ Travel discounts: www.ov-chipkaart.nl/travel-with-travel-products/national-travel-products.htm
→ Online train ticket: www.ns.nl/producten/producten/p/e-ticket
→ Students: www.ov-chipkaart.nl/apply-1/which-card-is-right-for-you/students.htm
→ Getting to and from the train station:
www.ns.nl/en/door-to-door
→ Traveling with functional disabilities: www.ns.nl/en/travel-information/traveling-with-a-functional-disability
→ Zone taxis: www.ns.nl/en/door-to-door/consumers/book-an-ns-zonetaxi.html
→ Prices, departure and arrival times: www.9292ov.nl

Cycling

During morning rush hour, the bicycle paths in the big cities become very dangerous as they can barely accommodate the number of cyclists and because these same cyclists are too focused on their cell phones. This is the conclusion of the Association for Scientific Research into traffic safety, based on research carried out in The Hague and Amsterdam.

In both cities, they set up cameras to study what was going on on four different bicycle paths and it became clear that 20 percent of the cyclists was on their cell phone. "Most of them listen to the radio or are talking on the phone. Only a few of them are actually typing, or holding the phone to their ear, but still, this constitutes sufficient distraction," says Director Peter van der Knaap.

English-Style

What they also noticed is that relatively many cyclists (5 percent) cycle in the wrong direction – also called 'English cycling', and that most of them (80 percent) do not look over their shoulder before making a move to pass another cyclist. This can cause serious accidents, the Association warns. These accidents have been registered by the cameras.

Utrecht, City Center

Van der Knaap indicates that serious measures are required. Such as widening the cycle paths on busy routes, so that also people who are using a cargo bike have a enough room to maneuver. "If necessary, at the expense of parking spots," says the Association.

This cycling behavior was studied during early morning rush hour in 2015. The Association says that it does not represent overall Dutch cycling behavior, but that it can be considered indicative of the behavior in other busy cities.

Bicycles, the Heart of Dutch Culture

A h, the bike, the Dutch bike, *de fiets*. Pity it wasn't invented in the Netherlands, for wouldn't it be a far better symbol of this nation than the tulip or the wooden shoe? It conjures up the very essence of Dutch culture, and I will tell you why.

Not all immigrants appreciate Dutch bikers, whichever background they may have. Foreign visitors find their behavior unpredictable, dangerous, and anarchistic – with bikers suddenly popping up when you least expect them. And I agree, it is all true, but let me take you along another line of thought which may be worth considering too...

To my idea, the Dutch bike – the simple, sturdy, run-of-the-mill black bike, omnipresent in Dutch cities – reflects several traditional Dutch characteristics.

Obviously, in a flat and very crowded country, it is a pragmatic means of transportation that gets you everywhere in no time, certainly when you ignore traffic signs and other silly official obstructions which, as a tax-paying citizen, you may question and toss aside. In applying a riding style that foreigners tend to describe as 'suicidal', a Dutch city biker will reach his/her destination far sooner than when using the tram, let alone a car.

Another plus: everyone can afford a bike, be it new or second-hand. Not generally employed in any status games, it is a very egalitarian means of transportation. As bikers are exposed to rain and wind and the laws of gravity on steep bridges, any difference in status or social stature between them is soon eradicated, revealing the essence of life: a body struggling against the forces of nature. Office clerk, bricklayer, human resources manager or secretary of state, all bikers have to bow to the elements. And toiling against gale force 8 on an unsheltered dike road or a straight-as-a-ruler suburban street will encourage modesty in anyone, making him equal to his fellow human beings who suffer likewise. Well, theoretically, that is.

The bike also satisfies the Dutch inclination to not waste any resources. It is not only a cheap means of transportation, it also improves one's general shape, thus reducing medical expenses. On a slightly more abstract level, bikers can also congratulate themselves on the fact that their effort is for the good of the planet as a whole: no fumes, no noise, no use of exhaustible resources, no great amount of unnaturally paved space needed. What could be more satisfying than a good conscience combined with excellent health and a well-filled wallet?

But that is not all. Riding a bike could be seen as having a touch of philosophy to it, even spirituality. It teaches the rider balance, and we're not only talking about physical balance. Riding along during rush hour at about 20 km/h among scores of other bikers doing likewise, all – well, most of them – waiting for the red light to turn green, trying to find a clear section of road to cross, cycling through the pouring rain... Things like that produce a certain equilibrium with your fellow bikers, peace of mind almost, to quote a Hindu term. It makes you realize the true size of your ego: just a small flame among many, hardly more than that of a match, nothing special really.

Besides balance, biking teaches you alertness. Though the race may not be about winning, it's challenging nonetheless: avoiding the carefully parking truck, calculating whether you can still pass just in front of that car that has no right whatsoever to be going so fast, racing for a minute to catch the bridge just before it closes (or is it: opens?) for a ship, catching the orange light nanoseconds before it turns red and when this fails, scanning the surroundings for any signs of police presence.

So with eyes on all sides and ears open to the sounds of car tires, tram bells, moped noises and of course each other's ringing bells, bikers wind their way through the ever-changing river of traffic where they may physically be the weaker party but morally speaking are superior by far: unpretentious, silent, un-polluting, utterly democratic, going with the flow and yet self-willed. This feeling of modest self-righteousness gets stronger when the bike is used for the transportation of items such as the daily shopping, the two children, a dog, or a pile of wood for some do-it-yourself job.

There are a thousand and one subtle effects and conditions which become part of your delicate existence when you bike. In a densely populated nation, give and take are essential, and biking may be a good preparation for the bigger podium of life. Royalty, prime ministers and captains of industry have preceded you, so what's keeping you from joining the steel-framed army when going to work, school or the supermarket? If you can't beat us, join us. See you at the traffic light!

Some Facts & Figures

→ There are about 23 million bicycles in Holland, making that more than one for every inhabitant

→ About 1.1 million new bicycles are sold every year

→ The Dutch cycle approximately 13.5 billion kilometers per year

→ The percentage of bicycle owners is the highest among those with the highest income

→ There are 2,615 bicycle shops in Holland

→ There are 37,000 kilometers of bicycle paths and lanes, and 116,500 kilometers of paved roads

→ In the provinces of Drenthe and Noord-Brabant there are relatively more cars, due to the fact that distances are greater and public transportation not quite as omnipresent

→ Conversely, the number of cars in the bigger cities is relatively low

→ 47 percent of the Dutch housholds has one car in front of their house. Almost 21 percent of the Dutch households have two or more cars, while fewer than one family in four does not have a car

→ Holland is the fourth safest country to drive in. Only the U.K., Sweden and Norway have lower numbers of fatalities

→ There are 5,046 kilometers of waterways navigable for ships of 50 tons

→ There are approximately 162,000 recreational boats in the Dutch harbors/water sports companies

→ In Drenthe, there are 1,000 recreational boats, in the provinces of North Holland and South Holland, there are 32,000 each

→ There are 3,200 kilometers of standard gauge railways

→ On average, the Dutch travel a little over 30 kilometers a day: 22.5 by car (either as a driver or a passenger), 3 by train and 2.5 by bike

→ 8.6 of these kilometers are work-related, 6 are for social purposes (visiting other people's homes), and 5.5 for sports, hobbies or going out

Driver's License

As a rule, residents of the Netherlands are required to have a Dutch driver's license in order to drive a motor vehicle. You are a resident if you spend at least 185 days per calendar year in the Netherlands.

Here are a few additional rules (or, as the case may be, exceptions):

→ If you have a driver's license that was issued in the countries listed in the box, you are entitled to drive in the Netherlands on it for 15 years after it was issued, unless it expires earlier, in which case you can use it until that date. This applies to licenses in categories that start with A through B. Those that start with C through D, can be driven on in the Netherlands for five years after they were issued.

→ If your license was issued more than 15 years ago, but still valid, you can drive on it another two years after registering in the Netherlands.

→ Once these periods have expired, you will have to get a Dutch driver's license – to which purpose you can exchange it. You can also opt to exchange it for a Dutch license straight away.

→ Licenses issued in the countries in the box *after* registering in the Netherland cannot be used here.

→ If you have a driver's license that was issued in any other country, you may drive in the Netherlands on your foreign license for a period of six months (185 days) after registering as a Dutch resident. During this period, you have to take a driving test in the Netherlands to acquire a Dutch driver's license

→ You cannot exchange a so-called international driver's license for a Dutch license, as it is merely considered to be a translation of the national driver's license.

Exchanging Your License

If you live in the Netherlands and have valid residential status you may trade in a valid driver's license issued by the countries listed in the box, as well as Aruba, Monaco, Isle of Man, Netherlands Antilles, and the State of Jersey for a Dutch license.

Driver's licenses issued in the following countries can be exchanged if they cover the categories listed here: Taiwan, B (passenger car); Israel, B (passenger car); Japan, IB (passenger cars and motorcycles of more than 400cc); Singapore, Class 2 (motorcycles of more than 400cc) and Class 3 (passenger car), Andorra (license for passenger cars); South Korea, second class ordinary license; the Quebec province of Canada, Class 5; and all categories of licenses from Aruba, Netherlands Antilles, Jersey, Isle of Man, and Monaco.

The procedure for exchanging your license can be found on the website listed below.

The 30%-Ruling

If you are benefiting from the 30% tax ruling, you and the other member(s) of your family can simply exchange your license,

provided it is still valid, no matter where you are from. Ask for an exchange form for your foreign driver's license at your local municipal office.

License Verification

The Department of Road Transport may ask you to have the validity of your driver's license and the significance of certain information confirmed by the Consulate or Embassy of the country that issued the foreign driver's license. You may also be required to have the content of the foreign driver's license translated by an approved interpreter/translator. For Japanese, Taiwanese and Chinese licenses, this is obligatory.

Certificate of Fitness/Medical Check-Up

You need a Certificate of Fitness (*Verklaring van Geschiktheid*) to prove that you are medically fit enough (physically and mentally) to drive a car. In some cases, you may have to undergo a medical examination. When, and how, to go about this, you can find on the website listed below.

Wind Mills along the IJsselmeer

Countries on whose license you are allowed to drive in the Netherlands for a period of ten years after issuance (or, if it is valid for a shorter period of time, until the expiration date): Austria, Belgium, Bulgaria, Croatia, (the Greek part of) Cyprus, Czech Republic, Denmark, Estonia, Finland, France, Germany, Greece, Hungary, Iceland, Ireland, Italy, Latvia, Liechtenstein, Lithuania, Luxembourg, Malta, Norway, Poland, Portugal, Rumania, Slovakia, Slovenia, Spain, Sweden, Switzerland, and the United Kingdom (including Northern Ireland). On a license issued in any other country, you are allowed to drive during a period of 6 months.

Special rules apply to those who have been accorded diplomatic or consular staff status, as well their families. Contact the RDW (Dutch Road Traffic and Transport Authority) or the Ministry of Foreign Affairs, Protocol Department, for more information.

You must be at least 18 years of age to drive a car in the Netherlands. There is one exception: 17-year-olds who already have a driver's license can drive accompanied by an adult who has officially been registered as their accompanier. The young driver is issued a special license, with the names of the approved accompaniers on it.

Return of Your Original Driver's License

The original driver's license will be returned to the embassy or country of origin of the license. Depending on the legislation of the country that has issued the license, you can then have it returned to you.

Taking the Driver's Exam

If your driver's license cannot be traded in, you will have to take a theory test and a road test at the Central Road Aptitude Bureau (*Centraal Bureau Rijvaardigheid*, or CBR).

You can take the Theory Exam in English. It takes one hour and consists of 65 multiple choice questions, 40 of which test your knowledge of the Dutch traffic rules (12 test your knowledge of the rules and 28 your insight into participating in traffic) and 25 of which test your recognition of, and response to, dangerous situations in traffic. Below we have listed two sites that can help you arrange driving lessons and the exam in English.

On www.traffictrainer.nl you can take theoretical practice exams in English.

Websites
→ General information: www.rdw.nl/over-rdw/
   information-in-english
→ Driving lessons in English: www.dutchdriverslicense.com
   Central Office for Motor Vehicle Driving Testing,
   CBR: www.cbr.nl

Health Care

Going to the Doctor

The GP

Ah yes... Your first sneeze. Your throat hurts. Time to do to the doctor... Or is it?

Beware: culture shock coming up! In the Netherlands, no one goes to the doctor for a cold. After all, with these wet and rainy winters, that have everyone sniffling their way through the day – if they all went to the doctor, he wouldn't have any time left! Or so the Dutch think. In general, they believe in seeing if whatever they have goes away of its own accord. And even if it's serious enough to warrant a visit to the GP, chances are he'll send you home with the advice to take it easy and drink lots of fluids... They're not much into any type of medication and certainly not antibiotics. There are even ads on the radio, aimed at dissuading the general public from poppin' them pills too frequently, warning us against the consequences of using them willy nilly.

But say you decide you want to go to a GP. First, you have to find one, which you can do by asking around among your colleagues, neighbors and friends to see whom they recommend. The GP is someone you have to feel comfortable with when you are at your least comfortable, so take your time and arrange to meet your new doctor, if that makes you feel more at ease.

For simple questions, or to request a refill for your prescription, most doctors have a *telefonische spreekuur*, whereby you can call in and speak to the doctor (or, at times, his assistant, who has followed special training) with your question or request.

Appointment

GPs have two types of appointment schedules: either one by which you call and make an appointment (usually for the same day, maybe the next) or they have *inloopspreekuur*, which means that the doors open at, say 8:00 A.M., and you can just walk in; first come, first serve. Expect your appointment to last not much longer than 10 minutes; if you think you'll want more time, ask for a double appointment. For non-office hour emergencies, you call your doctor's office and a voice recording will tell you who to contact. Increasingly, this is a so-called *huisartsenpost* (GP office) at the nearest hospital. In most cases, emergencies that require stitching or a cast can be dealt with by your GP or the SEH (*Spoedeisend Hulp*, Emergency Help) at a hospital. Not all hospitals offer SEH anymore, so be sure to find out before you race over there!

For the latest on Covid in the Netherlands — statistics, measures or risks — visit the English-language site www.rivm.nl/en/coronavirus-covid-19.

Seeing a Specialist

If you want to see a specialist, you can't just pick up the phone and call a hospital (which is from where most specialists work). You have to go to your GP first, and discuss your problem with him; ultimately, he will decide whether he thinks your problem is cause for referral. This sounds worse than it is; if you really want to see a specialist, just be adamant.

Next, make sure you hold on to the referral notice (*verwijsbrief*) your GP gives you. Once you've made your appointment, you will have to show it to the specialist's assistant as without it, your insurance company will not cover the expenses. Your appointment will probably be canceled if you don't bring it. International insurance policies (rather than local Dutch ones) may have different rules regarding specialist referrals, so consult your specific policy to be sure of what to expect.

There might be a waiting list, and if you speak Dutch, you can look these up on the site listed below. Else, you can ask your GP or a local friend if they can help you find out more.

The specialist will read the note provided by your GP, discuss your situation with you, arrange the necessary tests and prescribe a possible treatment. Probably, you will not be filling out four pages of your own (and your entire family's) medical history before the visit – but this really depends on your medical problem. If there is anything potentially of importance, be sure to mention it – such as former illnesses, hereditary afflictions and allergies to medication.

If this is your first visit to the hospital, you register at the front desk. There you will be asked a few questions (your name, address, insurer, GP, and a few other questions). This information will go into the computer and also onto a little credit card-sized plastic card, called a *ponsplaatje*, which you must bring with you every time you go to the hospital as it is used, among others, to find your records, mark forms, send your bills to your insurance company, and to print out labels for lab tests.

Some hospitals now make use of an electronic card, called the *electronische patiëntenpas*. Some hospitals have neither – so it is best to ask at the information desk the first time you go to the hospital.

Medication

If your GP or specialist decides you will need medication, he will give you a prescription (*recept*). If you live in a country where you leave the doctor's office with a prescription for at least three types of medicine no matter what you have, then you had best be prepared. As mentioned earlier, when it comes to your standard afflictions, Dutch doctors have great confidence in your immune system's ability to deal with your unwanted invaders

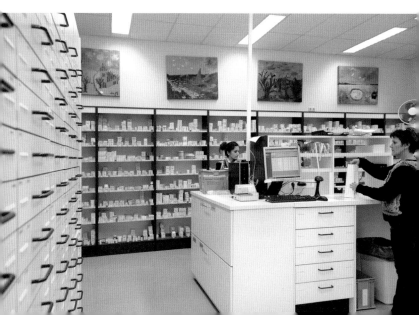

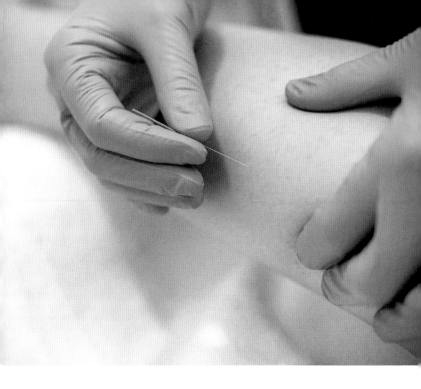

adequately. Of course, serious problems will be given serious attention and commensurate medication.

For insurance coverage, check our item on Health Care Insurance.

Prescription drugs are filled at an *apotheek* (pharmacy). They computerize your prescriptions and keep a close watch on the drugs you are taking in order to avoid drug interaction. Many bill your insurance company directly for the costs of prescription medicine.

Alternative Medicine

Alternative medicine such as acupuncture and homeopathy are also very popular in the Netherlands. For more information, get in touch with the *Alternatieve Geneeswijzen Infolijn* (website provided below). Homeopathic medicines can be purchased at either a pharmacy, a drugstore, or a health food store, and is generally not covered.

If you need physical therapy, manual therapy, haptonomy, chiropractics, (psychological) therapy, cranial-sacral therapy, or need other help with physical disabilities, or need advice on your sexual health, ask your GP for recommendations – don't forget the referral notice!

Emergencies

→ In case of an emergency, call the national emergency number 112.

→ State whether you need an ambulance, the police or the fire department and they will connect you with the right department

Websites

→ For general information on hospitals, including waiting lists: www.vzinfo.nl

→ Alternative medicine: www.infolijn-alternatieve-geneeswijzen.nl

Huisartsen (GP) search engines

→ www.huisartsen.nl

→ www.huisarts-gids.com

→ www.zorg.independer.nl/huisartsen

→ www.zorgkaartnederland.nl

To make an appointment for a Coronatest

→ www.coronatest.nl

Dental Care

→ www.tandarts.nl

→ www.tandarts.pagina.nl

→ www.tandartsplein.nl

So You're Pregnant... Congratulations!

There are many myths and legends surrounding pregnancy and child birth in the Netherlands. Here we deal with a number of them.

I will have to give birth at home.

MYTH Being the no-nonsense, medical-issues-are-merely-a-blip-on-the-road people they are, the Dutch definitely romanticize home births, stressing how at ease they will feel giving birth in their own bed/bathtub. Yet, only just over 12 percent of births take place at home. You might have been told that only home births are covered by your insurance, but also that is not true. If you have a medical conditioning warranting hospital birth, your insurance will fully cover the birth in the hospital. Also, you can opt for a *poliklinische bevalling*, in which case you go to the hospital when your contractions reach a certain frequency and leave within hours of the baby's birth. Most insurance companies cover this too. You might have to pay a contribution. Home birth-related costs are indeed fully covered.

I won't be able to go to a gynecologist; I will be treated by a midwife.

MYTH Most pregnant Dutch women go to a local midwife, who is also present when the baby is born. (Most midwifes share a practice. This means that you will not necessarily always see the same one on each visit and that the midwife who is on duty is the one who will be holding your hand when you give birth.) However, if you wish to go to a gynecologist, you can request this. Certainly if there are medical problems, you will be referred to one straight away. If the gynecologist deems this necessary, you will stay under their supervision.

If you have continuously been under midwife supervision, she will also be present should you decide to have your baby in the hospital. The advantage of the latter is that, now that you are in a hospital, a gynecologist will be close by in case of emergency.

I will have to give birth without painkillers.

MYTH You don't *have* to give birth without painkillers. Midwifes are generally not allowed to administer them, so if you give birth at home, you will have to make do without them – unless you try out acupuncture, TENS or hypnosis. If you give birth in the hospital, you have a variety of options: laughing gas, an epidural, remifentanil, and painkillers.

The midwife does not carry out any medical check-ups.

TRUTH Here's what they *do* do. They listen to the baby's heart; they monitor the baby's position; the growth of your uterus; your blood pressure; and, if they can't carry this out themselves, they send you to a specialist to do an ultrasound during your first or second visit, to verify the pregnancy, your progress and the number of babies inside.

You visit a midwife once every four weeks, during the first half of your pregnancy. After that, the frequency of the visits increases. Your midwife becomes your friend, someone who takes her time for all your questions, concerns, doubts and hopes, and she will always refer you to a gynecologist if you, or they, need more answers or reassurance.

Someone will come help me out the week after I give birth.

TRUTH This is called *kraamzorg* (maternity home care). The *kraamverzorgster* takes care of you and your baby and is a valuable source of information and reassurance who offers you practical tips on your recovery, the baby's development, nursing, bathing, safety when sleeping, pets, etc. Generally, she will make sure that you take care of yourself too, and will provide you with healthy food and time to take a nap.

You have a legal minimum right to a total of 24 hours of *kraamzorg*, spread over eight days, with the standard being 45 hours (49 if you are nursing) – though your insurance policy may cover, for instance, 80 hours over a maximum of ten days.

There is no prenatal testing.

MYTH The Dutch medical system offers prenatal screening and prenatal diagnostics to those who want it. It is not obligatory. Prenatal screening includes: testing your blood group and checking for possible STDs; the Combination Test that tests for Down's Syndrome (a combination of a blood test and a neck fold measurement); the Triple Test (to check for Down's Syndrome); and an ultrasound at 20 weeks' pregnancy. Prenatal diagnostics

are offered to pregnant women who are older than 36, and include Chorionic Villi Sampling (to check the chromosomes and DNA and test for genetic abnormalities); Amniocentesis (to tests for genetic abnormalities and the chances of Spina Bifida); additional ultrasounds; and NIPT (Non-Invasive Prenatal Test), to check for genetic abnormalities, and which can be used instead of Chorionic Villi Sampling or Amniocentesis.

TRUTH or MYTH?

I have a right to pregnancy leave.

TRUTH If you are (self-)employed, have a right to 16 weeks' paid leave surrounding the birth of your baby, which can be initiated between 4-6 weeks prior to the estimated due date. In fact, *you may not work* from four weeks before, until six weeks after delivery (not that anyone will be checking this if you are self-employed). If the baby is late, and you have used up the six weeks beforehand, you also still have a right to a ten-week leave following the baby's birth.

During pregnancy leave you receive 100 percent of your normal wages – either directly from the Social Security Institution or via your employer – up to a maximum of the so-called daily wage a day, though some employers pay out the gap between this and your full last-earned salary. For self-employed moms, the amount you receive depends on the number of hours you worked in self-employment the previous year.

TRUTH or MYTH?

Daddies/partners also get some time off.

TRUTH Dads/partners are entitled to a week's paid leave on the day the baby is born to stand by the mother right after birth. They have four weeks in which to take up this leave. If the dad/partner has to rush from work to stand by the mother as she gives birth, this is covered by so-called calamity leave or short-term leave.

After this, they have six months in which dads/partners can request a maximum of five weeks of additional leave. During this period, they receive 70 percent of their wages, to a maximum of 70 percent of the so-called daily wage.

I, or my husband, can take unpaid leave to take care of my children.

TRUTH At some point during the first seven years of your child's life, both of you can take unpaid leave of absence to care for your child (adoption or foster child included). In principle, the idea is that you work 50 percent during a period of one year, but as the rules are not always practical – for either the employee or employer – other conditions may be agreed upon. Both of you can do this at once, or one after the other. In the case of twins, you can take twice the amount of leave. Although not required by law, some employers continue to pay up to 75 percent of the wages during parental leave. As of 2022, nine of these weeks are paid – again, for twins, twice this amount of weeks. These nine weeks have to be taken up during the first year of the child's life (for adoption and foster children: inclusion in the family), and the parents receive 70 percent of their wages during this time. This paid leave is not available for self-employed persons.

Scheveningen Beach

The Dutch and their Pets

Pets have a position in Dutch households that is very similar to that of the children. Some are served the best cut of the rarest beef, others are given the best chair, with the best view of the TV – and, naturally, access to the accompanying snacks. And the care provided is top-notch: the veterinary services (a vet is called a *dierenarts*) are excellent in the Netherlands, and include animal hospitals, ambulances and even crematoriums. There are also dog-walking services (*honden uitlaat service*) for those who can't imagine life without Whoofy, but unfortunately have to spend the whole day in the office. And last but not least, the pet stores in the Netherlands offer a wonderful array of toys, cushions, cages, leashes, snacks, top-of-the-line food, and... pets, of course.

Finding a pet

If you want to buy a dog or cat, it is always better to do this via a recognized breeder rather than through a pet store. Breeders can be found through the Raad van Beheer op Kynologische Gebied in Nederland, the phone number of which you will find at the end of the chapter. For any other type of animal (other than the household rodent type – for which the pet store, or the petting farm, called *kinderboerderij*, will do fine) – you can best ask the local vet where you can find one. If you are looking to save an unwanted cat or dog, there are kennels, called *dierenasiel*, where 'lost and found' or otherwise homeless animals are brought. These kennels are well-run and most of the time have a good profile of the animals they are trying to place. Often, they have to find a new home for the pets of families who have to go abroad, or who have family member who is allergic to animals and find it greatly rewarding to have found such a loving pet a new home. And, of course, you can look on – for instance, Facebook – for organizations that place rescued pets from abroad up for adoption.

Dog tax

If you and your dog have been living in the Netherlands for a while, you might have been presented with a bill for dog tax. Not all municipalities levy it – a strange bit of inconsistency, but that's just one of those things – so it might not be an issue for you at all. In the past, civil servants would stroll through the neighborhood, ringing doorbells and asking whether you perhaps owned this barker, but nowadays this does not seem to be in anyone's actual job description anymore. This tax used to be a 'corporate' tax, but is now levied on private dog owners, the proceeds of which are used to create public dog parks, as well as doggy poop dispensers and receptacles. This is the only pet-related tax there is, so no need to worry about reporting your cat, rabbit or guinea pig!

Favorite Pets of the Dutch

1 Aquarium fish: 9.4 million
2 Fishing pond fish: 8.5 million
3 Cats: 3.9 million
4 Birds: 3.1 million
5 Dogs: 2.2 million
6 Chickens, Duck and Geese: 1.5 million
7 Rabbits: 1 million
8 Pigeons: 900,000
9 Rodents: 600,000
10 Reptiles and Amphibians: 250,000

Websites

Animal ambulance
→ www.dierenambulance.nl

Lost pets
→ To report lost animals: www.amivedi.nl

To (chip)registrate pets
→ Nederlandse Databank Gezelschapsdieren (NDG): www.ndg.nl

European pet network
→ www.europetnet.com

Index

Colophon

The Little Orange Handbook 2.0
The Netherlands for Newcomers

The first edition of *The Little Orange Handbook* was published in October 2016 (978 94 6319 014 5)

Publisher
XPat Media
Van Boetzelaerlaan 153, 2581 AR The Hague, the Netherlands
Tel: +31(0)70 306 33 10
e-mail: info@xpat.nl – internet: www.xpatmedia.nl

Editor
Stephanie Dijkstra

Contributing writers
Stephanie Dijkstra, Dutchnews.nl, Arnold Enklaar, Han van der Horst, Annebet van Mameren, Ana McGinley, Molly Quell, Hanneke Sanou, Jacob Vossestein

Graphic Design
Bram Vandenberge, igraph

Photography
Dawn Brown, Beeldbank Rotterdam, British School of Amsterdam, Ben Deiman, Depositphotos, Claire Droppert, Jonte van Essen, Iamsterdam, Bas de Meijer, Robert Oosterbroek, RVD, Shutterstock, The Hague Image Library, Karel Tomeï, Unsplash

Printed by
DZS Grafik

ISBN 978 94 6319 259 0 – NUR 600